SQL Backup and Recovery Joes 2 Pros®

Techniques for Backing up and Restoring Databases in SQL Server

By
Tim Radney
Founder TimRadney.com
Rick A. Morelan
Founder of Joes2Pros.com

©Tim Radney/Rick A. Morelan
All Rights Reserved 2012

ISBN: 1480127523
EAN: 978-1480127524

Table of Contents

About the Authors	5
Tim Radney	5
Rick A. Morelan	5
Acknowledgements from Tim Radney	6
Introduction	6
About this Book	7
Skills Needed for this Book	8
Software Needed for this Book	8
Chapter 1. File Backups	**9**
Full/Normal Backup	9
Incremental Backup	11
Differential Backup	13
Copy Backup	15
Summary	16
Points to Ponder File Backups	17
Review Quiz – Chapter One	19
Answer Key	20
Chapter 2. Database File Structures	**21**
Database File Structures	22
Impact of the Database Backup Process	32
Creating Databases	36
Summary	39
Points to Ponder Database File Structures	41
Review Quiz – Chapter Two	42
Answer Key	42
Chapter 3. Full SQL Backup	**43**
Using T-SQL	48
Restoring Using the Graphical UI	50
Restoring Using T-SQL	55
Summary	56
Points to Ponder - Full Backup	56
Review Quiz – Chapter Three	57
Answer Key	57

Chapter 4. Differential SQL Backups — 59
Using the Graphical UI — 60
Using T-SQL — 63
Restoring Using the Graphical UI — 64
Restoring Using T-SQL — 70
Summary — 71
Points to Ponder Differential Backup — 71
Review Quiz – Chapter Four — 72
    Answer Key — 73

Chapter 5. Transaction Log Backups — 74
Using the Graphical UI — 78
Using T-SQL — 82
Restoring Using the Graphical UI — 83
Restoring Using T-SQL — 89
Summary — 91
Points to Ponder Transaction Log Backup — 91
Review Quiz – Chapter Five — 93
    Answer Key — 93

Chapter 6. Common Restore Strategies — 94
Full Backup Only — 96
Full Backup with Differential Backups — 96
Full with Transaction Log Backups — 96
Full, Differential, Transaction Log — 98
Summary — 99
Points to Ponder Common Restore Strategies — 101
Review Quiz – Chapter SIX — 102
    Answer Key — 103

Chapter 7. Copy Backup — 104
Using the Graphical UI — 106
Using T-SQL — 109
Restoring a Copy Backup — 110
Summary — 110
Points to Ponder Copy Backup — 110
Review Quiz – Chapter Seven — 111
    Answer Key — 111

Chapter 8. File and Filegroup — 113
Using the Graphical UI — 119
Using T-SQL — 123
Restoring Using the Graphical UI — 124
Restoring Using T-SQL — 124
Summary — 129
Points to Ponder File and Filegroup Backup — 130
Review Quiz – Chapter Eight — 131
    Answer Key — 131

Chapter 9. Backing Up System Databases — 133
Restoring the Master Database — 134
Restoring the msdb Database — 137
Restoring the model Database — 138
Restoring the tempdb Database — 139
Summary — 140
Points to Ponder Backing Up System Databases — 141
Review Quiz – Chapter Nine — 142
    Answer Key — 142

Chapter 10. Additional Best Practices — 143
DBCC CHECKDB — 144
Backup Encryption — 144
What is Crash Recovery — 145
Instant File Initialization — 146
Summary — 146
Points to Ponder Additional Best Practices — 147
Review Quiz – Chapter Ten — 148
    Answer Key — 148
INDEX — 149

About the Authors

Tim Radney

In the mid-1990s Tim Radney found himself having to repair a Packard Bell 286 computer he received for Christmas the year before. Little did he know that learning to fix his own computer would be the beginning of his career. While in college he started repairing computers on the side, which led to him starting his own company. In 1998 he began working for a large southeastern financial company where he still works today. During his 14 years he served many roles from providing tier two support to becoming a senior systems administrator with dozens of certifications. As luck would have it, one day the CTO approached Tim to see if he would be interested in joining the database administration team. Tim jumped at the opportunity and has not regretted a moment of it. Within a short time he moved from a Jr. DBA to managing the team of system DBAs. Tim credits the SQL community for his success as a DBA.

Rick A. Morelan

In 1994, Rick Morelan could be found braving the frigid waters of the Bering Sea as an Alaska commercial fisherman. His computer skills were non-existent at the time. Such beginnings seemed unlikely to lead him down the path to SQL Server expertise at Microsoft. However, every computer expert in the world today woke up at some point in their life knowing nothing about computers. They say luck is what happens when preparation meets opportunity. In the case of Rick Morelan, people were a big part of his good luck.

Making the change from fisherman seemed scary and took daily schooling at Catapult Software Training Institute. Rick got his lucky break in August 1995, working his first database job at Microsoft. Since that time, Rick has worked more than 10 years at Microsoft and has attained over 30 Microsoft technical certifications in applications, networking, databases and .NET development.

Acknowledgements from Tim Radney

First I have to give recognition to my wife Theresa who is my biggest fan. She inspires me like no one ever has. Our journey together began when we were put on the same project at work and we met for the very first time. We became very good friends and our relationship grew from there. We have three amazing kids that keep us on the go. Also a big shout out to my parents who have always encouraged me to do my best and provided me with my first computer that started my journey.

Big thanks to the entire SQL Community, without you all I would be completely lost in this journey. There have been a number of people who have helped me along the way during my career in IT but in the past few years as a DBA there are a few that really stand out. Each of the following has given me key career changing pieces of advice, Aaron Nelson, Andy Leonard, Brian Moran, Jon Boulineau, Jorge Segarra, Jose Chinchilla, Karla Landrum, Mike Walsh, and Robert Pearl.

Last, but definitely not least, my friend and publisher Rick Morelan who has given me the amazing opportunity to write this book.

Introduction

Certain things in life we are expected to know how to do by instinct. Things such as involuntarily blinking our eyes when they need moisture, breathing without having to tell our body to take a breath, and knowing not to step out in front of a moving bus.

As a database administrator there are certain skills that we are expected to know and know extremely well. Two of those skills are making backups and performing restores. Backups and restores are the core foundation of a DBA's job. If a DBA is not protecting the data assets of the organization then there could be serious issues down the road that could ultimately cause the business to fail.

There have been countless stories told and questions posted to forums where database administrators have had server crashes only to find out that they did not have backups. Other posts report of DBAs who have been making backups only to find out that the backups are not valid when they tried to restore a failed database.

In some cases it has been reported that a legitimate backup solution was built out that included full, differential, and transaction log backups however the recovery solution did not meet the requirements of the business. In these cases, when the DBA had to perform a full restore of the server, too much time had passed and it caused irreversible damage to the company's reputation and the business had to close its doors.

Let this book guide you and get you to thinking about how you should be backing up your production servers and most importantly, how you would recover the databases in each situation.

About this Book

This book is designed to help the beginner and mid-level DBA to get a strong understanding of the types of backups available within SQL Server and how to restore each of those backups.

In this book we will cover each of the backups and then go over several common restore scenarios. This book includes examples to gain practical experience performing the different backup and restore techniques.

Working in the IT industry we are thrust into stressful situations constantly. We learn many skills on the job while we are in these stressful situations. The one skill that you do not need to learn in a crisis is how to recover your database. Being able to restore and bring a database online should be basic knowledge for us. It is our hope that upon reading this book and following along with the exercises you will be very comfortable with restoring any type of backup.

Skills Needed for this Book

This book is designed as a focused specialized lesson in good practice for backing up a database. Most readers of this book should be familiar with SQL and its general functions as well as how to navigate the object explorer and at least have basic T-SQL skills. Many readers may also have done many types of backups but wish to know more about all types of backups and when and how to use them together. You can be a beginner at SQL Administration or SQL Development as long as you are at an intermediate level in the other one. So welcome SQL Admins and Devs to getting your backup skills ready.

Software Needed for this Book

You will need to have a system with SQL Server installed. We recommend SQL Developer as the lowest cost way to be able to do every example in this book. Rather than going through a sea of software you can find a link to a $60 version of SQL Developer in the "Buy Now" section of the Joes 2 Pros web site. If you use SQL Express then about 20% of the labs and examples will not work for you.

Chapter 1.   File Backups

Backing up data is one of the most basic concepts in the computer world. Anyone that has ever lost family photos or important documents to either computer failure or human error knows the importance of a regular backup strategy. Failing to perform regular backups not only puts family memories at risk but can also cost a company a lot of money and man hours to rebuild an unrecoverable system.

Even though backing up data is a basic concept in terms of whether or not it should be done, it can seem like a complicated process to perform. Imagine we backed up all our important files last night containing everything we have ever worked on. Today we changed three files and don't want to lose our work. We could back up all the files again or maybe just the three that changed. When it comes to backups there are several choices.

It is important to understand that there are many different ways to backup a system, each with its own purpose. This chapter is designed to create a basic understanding of the most common types of backup methods. It will explain some of the uses for each type of backup along with some benefits and drawbacks of each. This chapter will not make someone an expert but will provide the understanding needed to start becoming a pro.

Full/Normal Backup

Merriam-Webster defines the term Backup [verb]: to make a copy of (a computer file or data) to protect against accidental loss; also Backup [noun]: a copy of computer data (as a file or the contents of a hard drive). In the SQL world a full backup is also referred to as a Normal Backup. A full database backup backs up the whole database. Full database backups are a compressed image of the database at the time the backup was completed.

Take a moment and look at Figure 1.1. Each night there is a backup performed. During the day files have been modified. To play it safe we backed up the whole file set on Sunday night before the work week started. On Monday during the day file 2 was worked on. File 2 will then raise its marker or flag to signal itself to be backed up Monday night. Since we are running a full backup every night we will again back up the entire set on Monday night to a storage device. Once the backup is done the marker is taken down indicating file 2 has been backed up. A full backup backs up the entire file set whether the flags are up or not. Once done, the full backup will reset all the markers. If the full backup is performed daily it uses the maximum storage space since the entire file set is backed up every day and not just the accessed files which may contain changes.

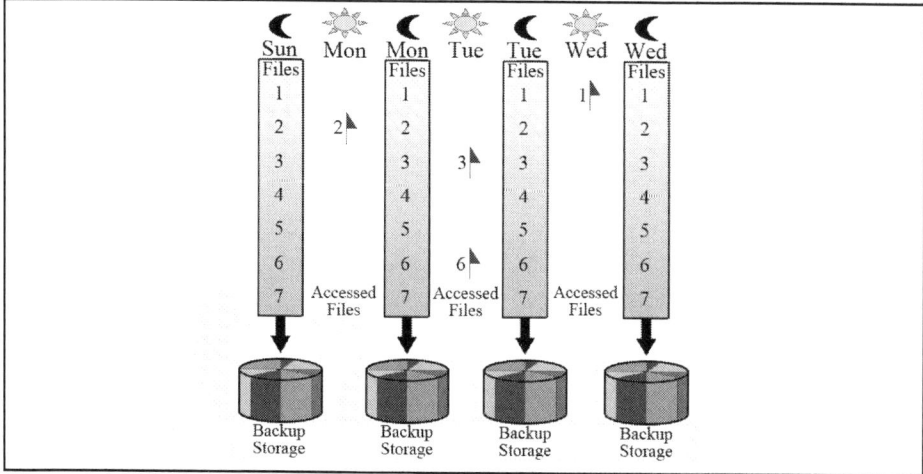

Figure 1.1 This shows full backups done each night with flags indicating accessed files from the work day.

READER NOTE: *In SQL Server these backup markers are called differential bitmaps since they detect differences in data instead of files.*

Figure 1.2 shows a crash on Thursday morning. Since a full backup was performed on Wednesday night nothing more is needed. If we are doing normal/full backups every night, we only need to restore the most recent full backup to recover all of the files.

Chapter 1 File Backups

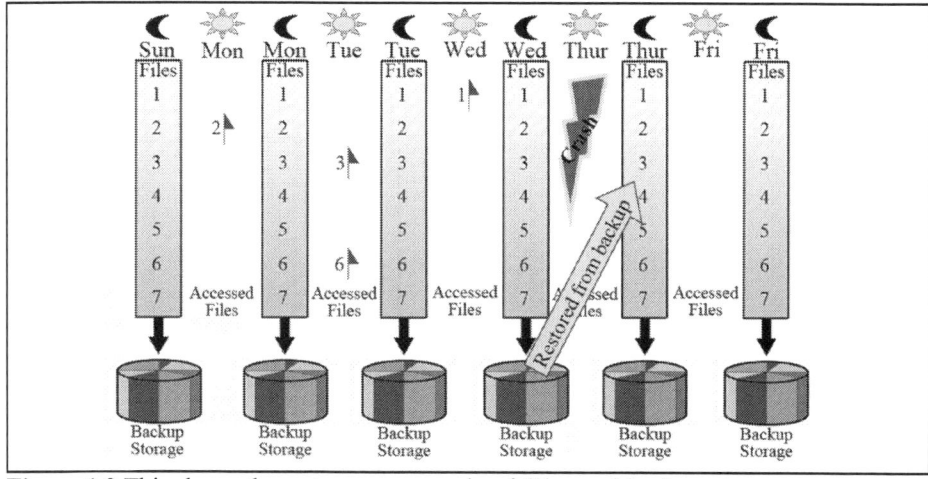

Figure 1.2 This shows the restore process using full/normal backups.

Full backups have the following features: All files are backed up completely; and all file flags are reset; the entire drive is backed up whether it changed or not.

Incremental Backup

Incremental [adverb] is defined as: occurring in small steps. An incremental backup would back up only those files that have been accessed and may contain changes.

Chapter 1 File Backups

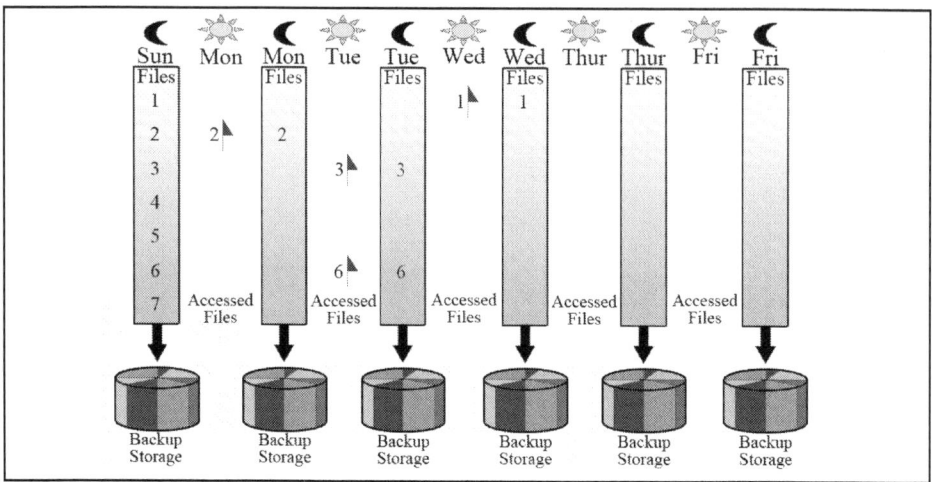

Figure 1.3 This Shows incremental backups of accessed files, flags removed with successful backup.

Take a moment and look at Figure 1.3 and compare it to the previous figures. What is different between the full backup and the incremental backup? On Sunday night before the work week started a full backup was performed. On Monday during the day file 2 was accessed. File 2 will then raise its marker or flag to signal itself to be backed up Monday night. After being backed up the marker is reset so it's not backed up again. Tuesday during the day, files 3 and 6 are altered and their markers rose because a change in these files has been detected. Therefore Tuesday night both file 3 and 6 will be backed up. The markers are reset once the backup for Tuesday night is successful. File1 is incrementally backed up the same way on Wednesday.

If we had a crash on Thursday morning, we would need the full backup from Sunday and incremental backup from Monday for file 2, Tuesday for files 3 and 6, and Wednesday for file1. Incremental backups only back up the flagged files. Once the backup is complete the flags are reset. The incremental backup uses the least amount of storage space but is more intensive to restore since all the incremental backups are needed.(Figure 1.4)

Chapter 1 File Backups

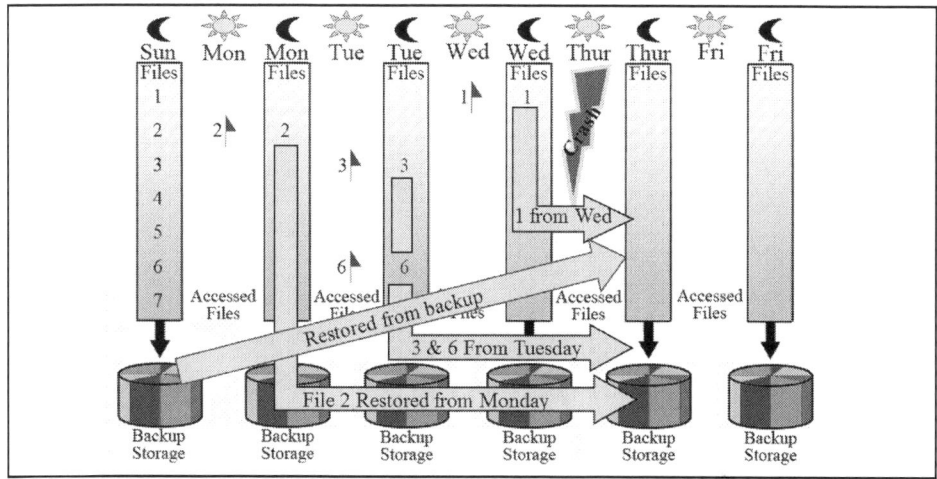

Figure 1.4 This shows the restore process from a full backup and many incremental backups.

Differential Backup

Differential [adjective] is defined as: Constituting a difference, making a distinction between. Take a look at Figure 1.5 and notice the differences with a differential backup. Again, a full backup was performed on Sunday night before the work week started. On Monday during the day file 2 was worked on. File 2 then raised its marker or flag to signal itself to be backed up Monday night. Here is where a differential backup differs from an incremental. After the backup is complete the marker is left up. Tuesday during the day files 3 & 6 are altered. Their markers go up because a change in these files is detected. Tuesday night both files 3 and 6 will be backed up along with file 2 since its flag was left up. Once the backup for Tuesday night is successful the markers again are left up. This process means that on Wednesday night, files 1 and 2 will be backed up because they were altered. In addition files 3 and 6 will also be backed up since their markers are still showing. Each day the differential backup set gets bigger until the next Sunday when the full backup finally resets all the flags again.

Chapter 1 File Backups

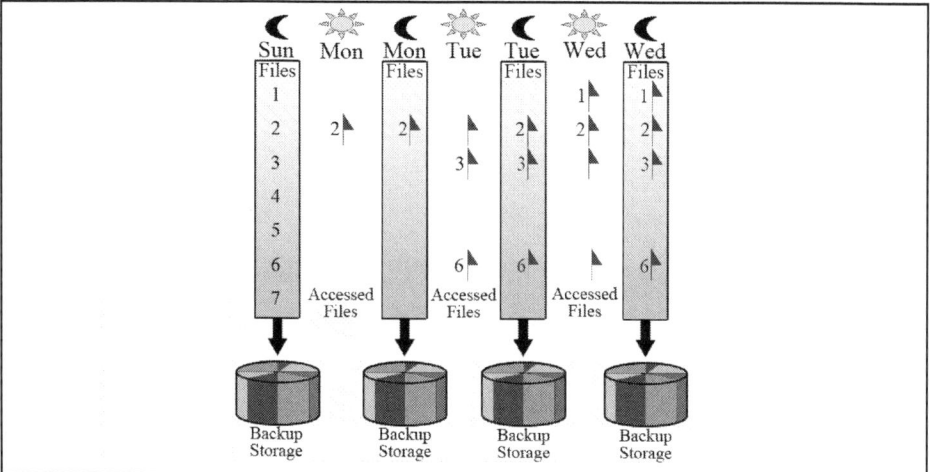

Figure 1.5 This shows differential backups with persisting flags after successful backup.

Thursday morning continues to be plagued by calamity. A full backup from Sunday and the differential backup from Wednesday are required to restore the system. Sunday has all the changes from the previous week and Wednesday has all the altered files for the week shown in Figure 1.6.

Differential backups have the following characteristics:
- o All flagged files are backed up
- o The flags (SQL Server calls them differential bitmaps) are not reset following a successful differential backup
- o All accessed files will be backed up with every backup
- o They are easier to restore after a crash, since we only need 2 backup file sets (the full backup file and the most recent full and differential backup files)

Chapter 1 File Backups

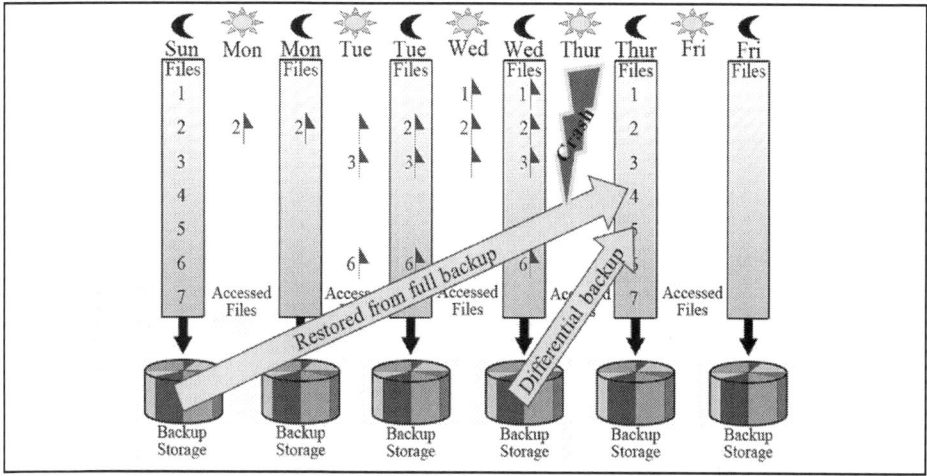

Figure 1.6 This shows the restore process from differential backups.

Copy Backup

What is the danger in doing a full backup in the middle of the week? The differential backup from Thursday will be a lot smaller than it was on Wednesday. If we did this backup and not everyone knew about it then another Admin doing Sunday's full and Thursday's differential would get an error. We don't do full backups in the middle of a backup cycle since it resets all the flags and throws off the schedule of the other types of backups.

What about a backup that does the entire set just like a full but does not reset the flags when it has completed. This is called a copy backup. This is a good option if we are worried about a mid-week failure and want to back up everything. This will allow us to make a safe copy without disrupting the week's backup system. We can run a copy backup in the middle of the week without resetting our markers and disrupting the weekly routines normally set by the differential or incremental. The copy backup will not upset the flag system since it ignores the flags when backing up and does not reset them once completed.

Chapter 1 File Backups

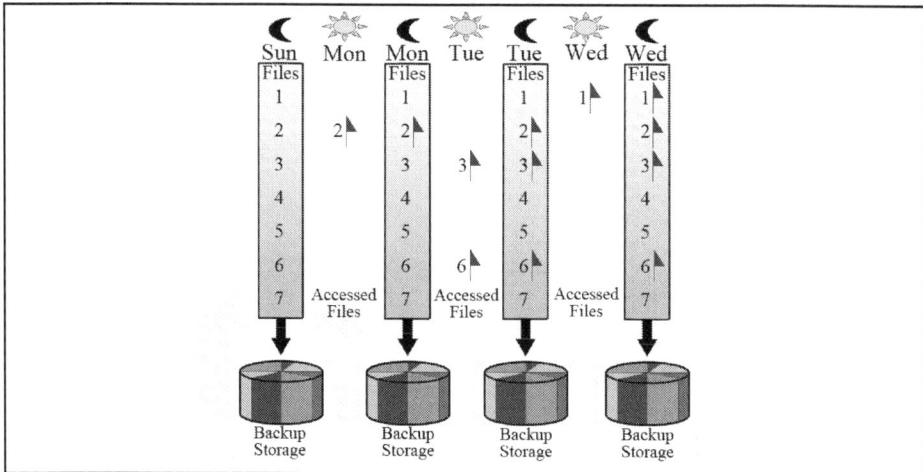

Figure 1.7 This shows copy backup does not remove flags following a successful backup.

A copy backup has the following characteristics: It's like a full backup without resetting the file flags. It is a safe option for a backup during the week.

Summary

The most robust backups are the full and copy. They use the most storage space. The copy backup is especially useful in a system test because it allows a full restore without interfering with scheduled differential backups. The copy backup can be maintained with as little as one backup file.

The most complete backup is the full/normal backup. It completely backs up all files and resets the markers of the altered files. The full backup is used for the weekly backup and leaves a clean slate for the upcoming week. The full backup can also be maintained with only one backup file.

The incremental backup is a good choice for frequent backups. The benefit of the incremental backup is that it utilizes very little storage space. The drawback however is that it can be cumbersome during the restore process. Each subsequent day from the full backup has to be restored

Chapter 1 File Backups

individually. The incremental backup method is maintained with a separate backup file for each incremental backup since the last full backup.

The differential backup is also a good choice for daily backups. It uses more storage space than the incremental backup but is much less cumbersome to restore. The differential backup can be maintained with as little as two backup files.

Backup Type	Backs up	Resets Marker
Full/Normal	Entire Set	Yes
Incremental	Only Marked Files	Yes
Differential	Only Marked Files	No
Copy	Entire Set	No

Figure 1.8 Side by side comparison of each backup type.

Backup Type	Backs up	Resets Marker
Full/Normal	Entire Set	Yes
Incremental	Only Marked Files	Yes
Differential	Only Marked Files	No
Copy	Entire Set	No

Figure 1.9 Side by side comparison of backup type system.

Points to Ponder
File Backups

1. Backing up critical data is a very important task for any network administrator.
2. A full backup does a backup of the entire set and resets any of the markers used by other backups.
3. An incremental backup will back up only the marked files and resets the markers.
4. The differential backup will back up only the marked files and will not reset the markers.

5. The copy backup is like a full backup that does not reset any of the markers.

Review Quiz – Chapter One

1.) The policy is to perform a full backup every Sunday night and incremental backups every weeknight. It is discovered on Wednesday morning that the system is corrupted and needs to be restored. Which backups are needed?

   O a. Just the latest full backup from Sunday.
   O b. Just the latest incremental backup from Tuesday.
   O c. The latest full and the latest incremental from Tuesday.
   O d. The latest full and both Monday and Tuesday incremental backups.

2.) The policy is to perform a full backup every Sunday night and differential backups every weeknight. It is discovered on Wednesday morning that the system is corrupted and needs to be restored. Which backups are needed?

   O a. Just the latest full backup from Sunday.
   O b. Just the latest differential backup from Tuesday.
   O c. The latest full and the latest differential from Tuesday.
   O d. The latest full and both Monday and Tuesday differential backups.

3.) What types of backups do not reset the backup markers?

   ☐ a. Full
   ☐ b. Copy
   ☐ c. Incremental
   ☐ d. Differential

Answer Key

1.) We want to restore up to Tuesday so (a) only gets us to Sunday and is incorrect. An incremental restore can only be done if the first restore is a full making (b) incorrect. The incremental backups need to be done in order until the last one. Since there are two incremental backups there will need to one full restore and two incremental restores making (d) the correct answer.

2.) We want to restore up to Tuesday so (a) only gets us to Sunday and is incorrect. A differential restore can only be done if the first restore is a full making (b) incorrect. For differential restores you only need to use one of them (the most recent) making (c) the correct answer.

3.) The full backup resets the markers making (a) incorrect. The differential and copy backup does not reset the markers making (b) and (d) both correct.

Chapter 2. Database File Structures

When a new database is created, it contains no data. In fact, it has no tables to hold data until we create them as well. Data is like cargo – it needs a container to hold it. The container itself is not really data, but a design or definition.

To put it plainly, this chapter is about how SQL handles the Server database storage for each database. SQL Server databases consist of files which are stored on a hard drive. Actually, I should qualify that – at least 80% of readers are probably like me and the "server" which their instance of SQL Server runs on is their local hard drive. (There may be a few developers who have a network set up and who are already running SQL Server on a separate machine or disk drive.) I have several machines, but I have one dedicated laptop I use for my Joes 2 Pros work.

***READER NOTE:** For the exercises in this chapter a folder needs to be created called Backups on the local C: drive (C:\Backups). Please run the script SQLBackupSetup01.sql in order to follow along with the examples for this chapter. All scripts mentioned in this chapter may be found in the "Solution Series" section at www.Joes2Pros.com.*

Database File Structures

Our first topic examines database file structures and how we can customize those available structures and settings to best fit our data traffic and system performance needs.

Let's begin with JProCo. Begin by dropping this database to see what the server (i.e., the hard drive) looks like without the JProCo database. Before and after we re-create this database, we will look at the hard drive to see the net impact of the JProCo database on my system.

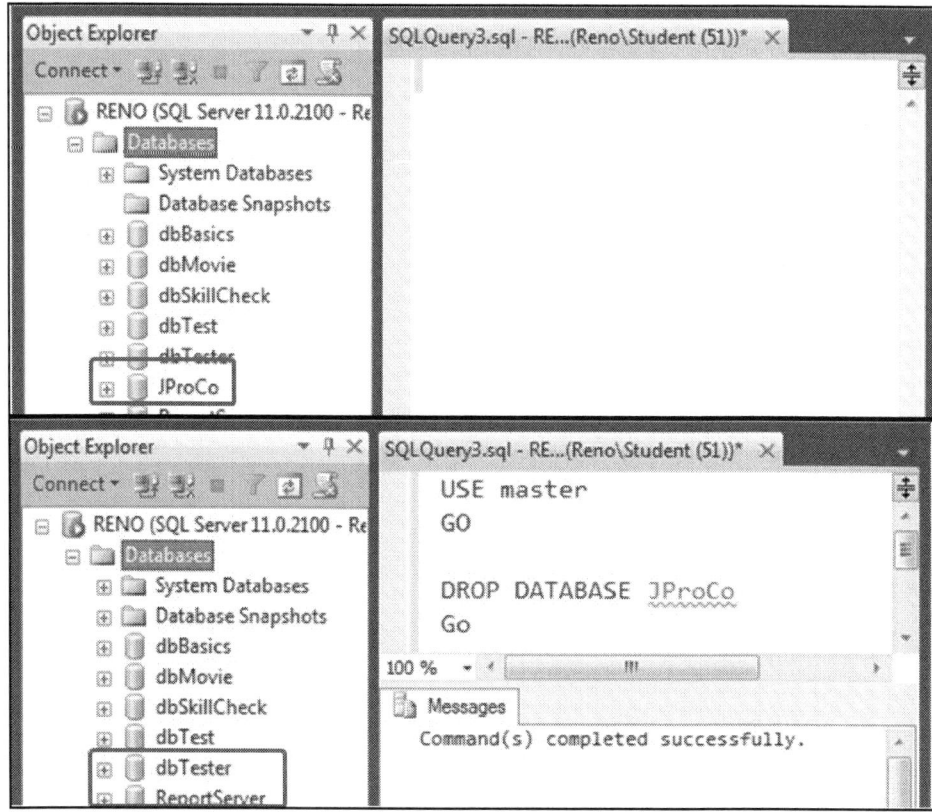

Figure 2.1 *Upper figure:* The JProCo database is shown in Object Explorer before it is dropped. *Lower figure:* JProCo is removed and confirmed in Object Explorer as gone.

Be aware that the Object Explorer tree does not dynamically update a database object after it is added or dropped. Expect to run this same refresh process each time Object Explorer is checked to see the updated changes in the list.

Now that JProCo has been removed, let's look at this hard drive and its current capacity.

To find capacity details on a machine, open Windows Explorer (**Windows Key + E**) > right-click the **C** drive > **Properties**.

It appears that this system has 499 MB free on the hard drive without the JProCo database. (Figure 2.2)

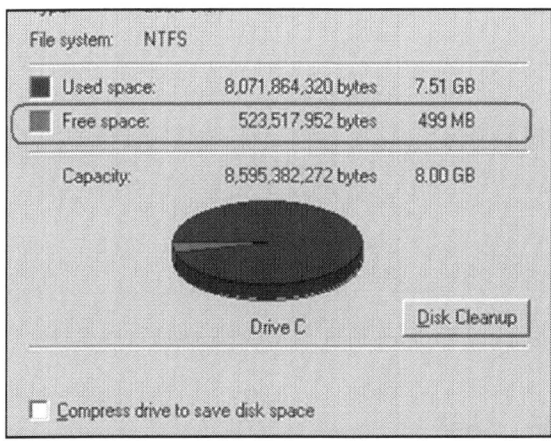

Figure 2.2 I have 499 MB free without the JProCo db.

Now rerun the setup script (SQLBackupSetup01.sql) to load the JProCo database onto my system fully populated. (Figure 2.3, Panel A). Once the script has executed successfully, go to SQL Server's **Object Explorer** > right-click the **Databases** folder > and choose **Refresh**. (Figure 2.3, Panel B). After the refresh, the JProCo folder becomes visible in my Object Explorer. (Figure 2.3, Panel C)

Chapter 2 Database File Structures

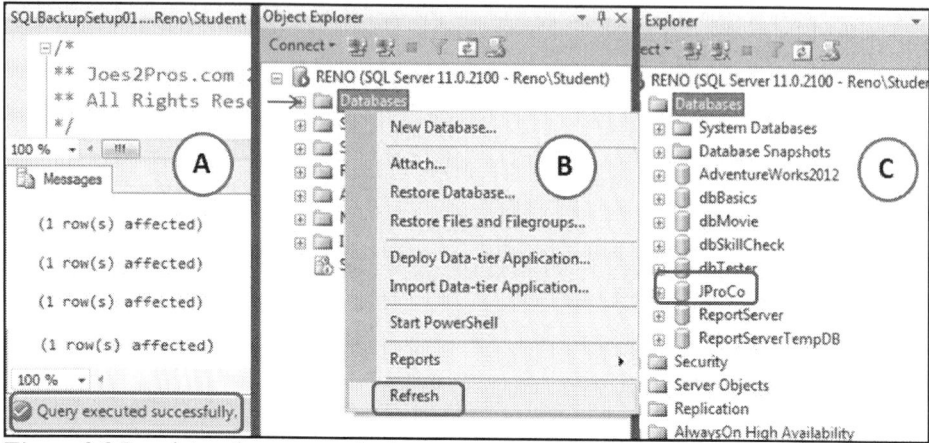

Figure 2.3 Panel A – the setup script has run successfully. Panel B – the Databases folder is refreshed. Panel C – the JProCo database becomes visible in Object Explorer.

Now return to the hard drive. Recall it showed 499 MB of free space prior to reloading the JProCo database onto the system. With JProCo now reloaded on this system it shows just 305 MB of free space. (Figure 2.4) So it appears JProCo is occupying roughly 200 MB someplace on the local drive.

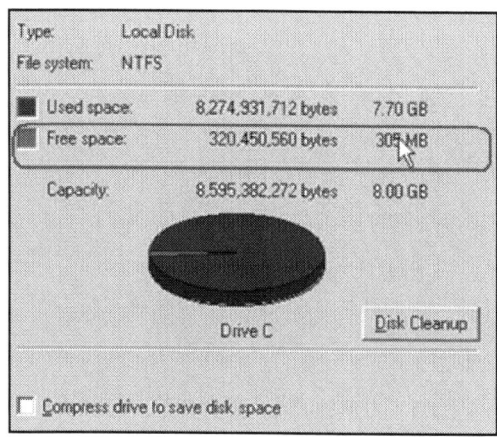

Figure 2.4 Just 305 MB of space is now free.

SQL Server chooses a default location to store databases whenever an alternate location is not specified. The file path shown here and in Figure 2.5 is the default location for SQL Server 2012:

Chapter 2 Database File Structures

C:\Program Files\Microsoft SQL Server\MSSQL11.MSSQLSERVER\MSSQL\DATA

This is the default location for SQL Server 2008:

C:\Program Files\Microsoft SQL Server\MSSQL10.MSSQLSERVER\MSSQL\DATA

Name	Date modified	Type	Size
AdventureWorks2012_Data	10/9/2012 1:00 AM	SQL Server Databa...	193,536 KB
AdventureWorks2012_log	10/9/2012 10:08 AM	SQL Server Databa...	768 KB
dbBasics	10/9/2012 11:23 AM	SQL Server Databa...	3,136 KB
dbBasics_log	10/9/2012 11:23 AM	SQL Server Databa...	832 KB
dbMovie	10/9/2012 11:23 AM	SQL Server Databa...	3,136 KB
dbMovie_log	10/9/2012 11:23 AM	SQL Server Databa...	832 KB
dbSkillCheck	10/9/2012 11:23 AM	SQL Server Databa...	2,112 KB
dbSkillCheck_log	10/9/2012 11:23 AM	SQL Server Databa...	528 KB
dbTester	10/9/2012 11:23 AM	SQL Server Databa...	2,112 KB
dbTester_log	10/9/2012 11:23 AM	SQL Server Databa...	528 KB
JProCo	10/9/2012 11:23 AM	SQL Server Databa...	152,448 KB
JProCo_log	10/9/2012 11:23 AM	SQL Server Databa...	45,632 KB

Figure 2.5 My MSSQL\DATA folder shows two JProCo files.

This screen capture of my MSSQL\DATA folder shows the two files which comprise the JProCo database. When I ran the setup script, SQL Server loaded these two files onto my system.

Notice that one file is roughly 152 MB in size (JProCo.mdf). The other file is roughly 45 MB (JProCo_log.ldf). Together they total roughly 200 MB – the same amount which we estimated JProCo occupies on my hard drive. These two files stored on the hard drive contain all of the data and all of the logging activity for the JProCo database.

DataFiles and LogFiles

At first many students do not find the concept of datafile and logfile activity an intuitive one. So we will ease into it with an example that helps

Chapter 2 Database File Structures

people grasp this topic quickly. But first we need a little explanation as to why SQL Server uses logfiles.

Ok, now we're ready to tackle datafiles and logfiles. Suppose that changes have been made to JProCo's Employee table. If we could peek into the datafile, we would find data identical with the result of SELECT * FROM Employee. However, it wouldn't tell us that an hour ago we deleted an employee record, or that today at 9:45 a.m. the manager added a new employee record to the table.

We can compare the datafile to getting information from the ATM. The data the ATM shows always provides my current balance very rapidly. But if we need to look back and see deposit or withdrawal information, the ATM can't help me. To see the transaction detail which has led to the current account balance, we need to look elsewhere.

Logfiles are just like the transaction history shown in bank statements, where we can find a separate transaction entry for every fee, deposit, or withdrawal made. The two identically structured WordPad files shown here (Figure 2.6 and Figure 2.7) are going to help us visualize the transaction activity retained by the logfile.

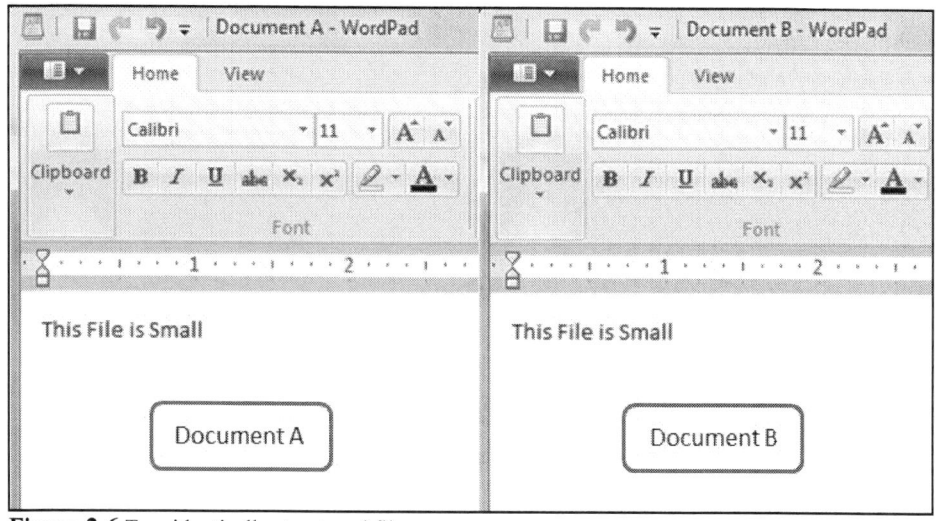

Figure 2.6 Two identically structured files.

Chapter 2 Database File Structures

These are pretty small files, just 1 KB each. We will make some significant edits to Document A, which we won't make to Document B. Not only will the documents differ visually, but when we see that the changes cause Document A's size to expand to 6 KB, it's clear that Document A and Document B are no longer identical files.

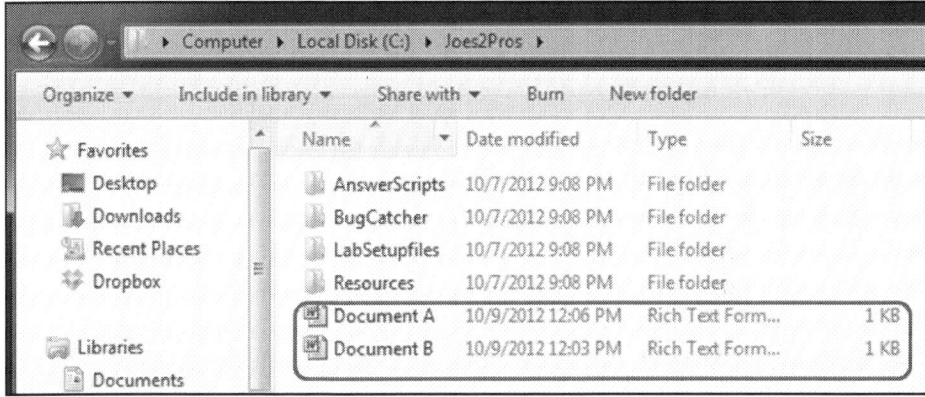

Figure 2.7 Documents A & B begin as identical files.

Where people tend to find the "ah-ha" moment is when we actually see the changes in Document A being removed one by one using the **Edit** > **Undo** to backtrack and see the edits disappear until they are both the same size again. In other words they were both small, then we added massive data to Document A and removed it again until they are again the same size.

Similarly, if we delete a few words one by one, the "Undo" operation will backtrack and each word reappears one by one. When we undo, we take back the most recent changes. How does the document know what the recent changes where? It must be logging that somewhere. What the application is doing is traversing through the log of changes and accessing memory to find all of those changes.

Chapter 2 Database File Structures

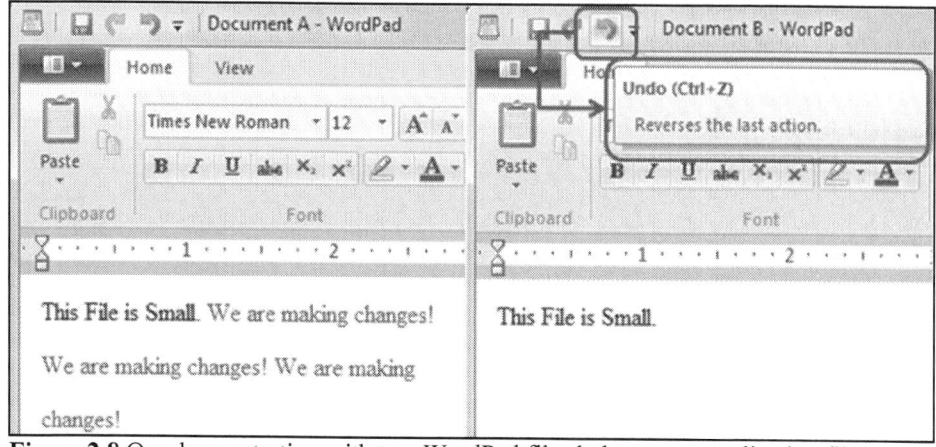

Figure 2.8 Our demonstration with two WordPad files helps conceptualize log file activity.

At the end Document A has been returned to its beginning state – it contains the identical information as Document B. Thus, Document A and B each are 1 KB in size at the end. But just prior to saving Document A, we make another interesting "ah-ha" observation. On the surface, both documents appear identical as shown in Figure 2.9. However, when we compare the size of the two files, Document A is many times larger than Document B. The log tracks changes made to the document from the last time it was saved up until the current moment.

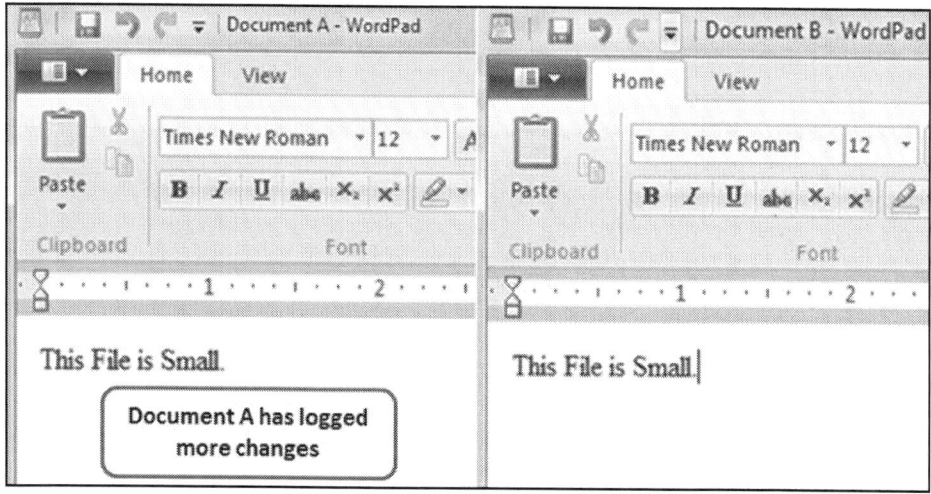

Chapter 2 Database File Structures

Figure 2.9 The log tracks all the changes from the last document backup (save) until now.

When the document gets saved it clears out the log and we can't undo anymore. We also get a nice reference point to regular server backups, which truncate (empty) the logfile. Document A's condition at the beginning and end of the demo (i.e., 1 KB and reflecting the data "This File is Small.") serves as a comparison to the datafile. Because the file was saved at the beginning of the demo and then again at the end, the document showed just the current state of the data – nothing to do with tracking data which was added or deleted along the way. The datafile's purpose is to reflect the current state of the database.

For student readers still trying to get their heads around this idea of datafiles and logfiles, have no fear –the next four pages include a step by step tutorial following data through the datafile and logfile as it enters a new database.

Step 1. Pretend we have a brand new database with one table (Employee) which contains zero records. There are no records in the JProCo database, so there are no records in the datafile. And since we haven't made any changes to the database, there are zero records in the logfile.

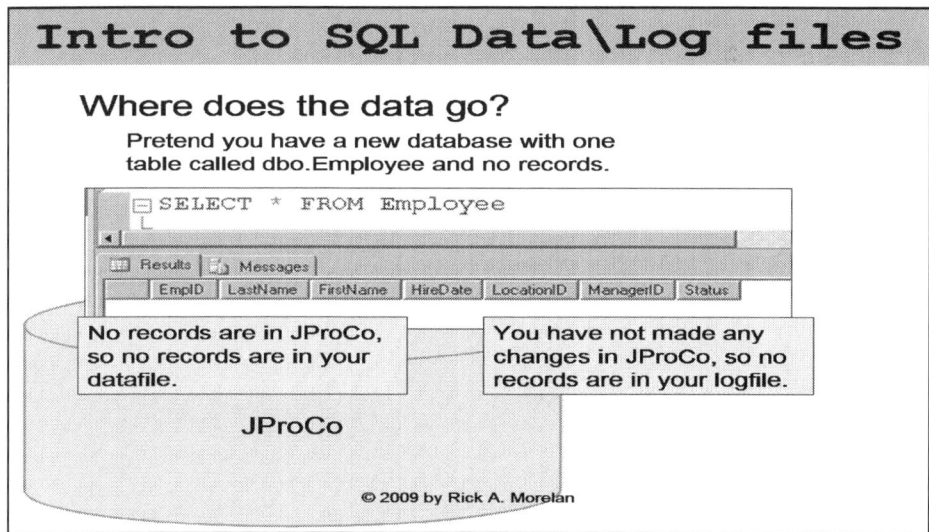

Figure 2.10 The brand new database contains zero records.

Step 2. Now data starts coming into the JProCo database. We add one new record for Alex Adams to the Employee table. So now we have one record in the datafile and one record in the logfile.

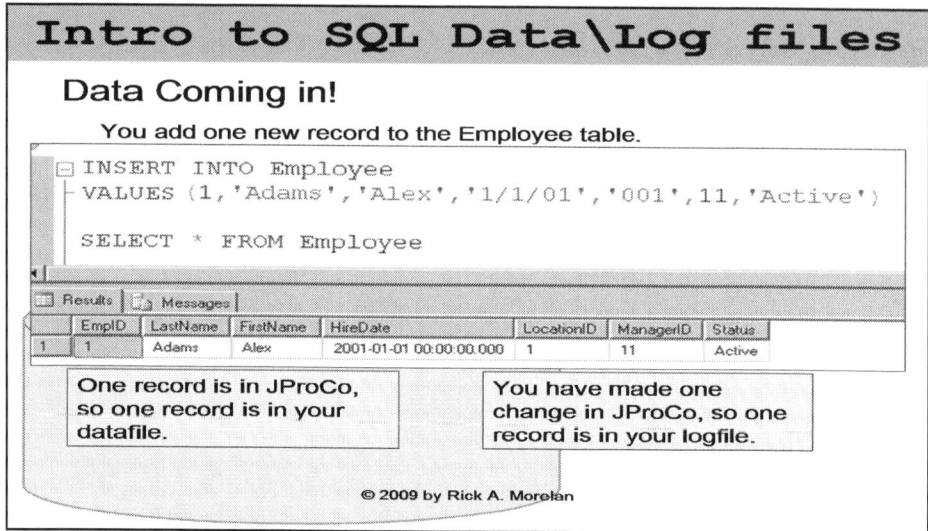

Figure 2.11 One record now appears in the database.

Step 3. We then add another record (Barry Brown). Two records are now in JProCo, so two records are in the datafile and two records in the logfile. So we have two pieces of data and two entries in the logfile reflecting those changes.

Chapter 2 Database File Structures

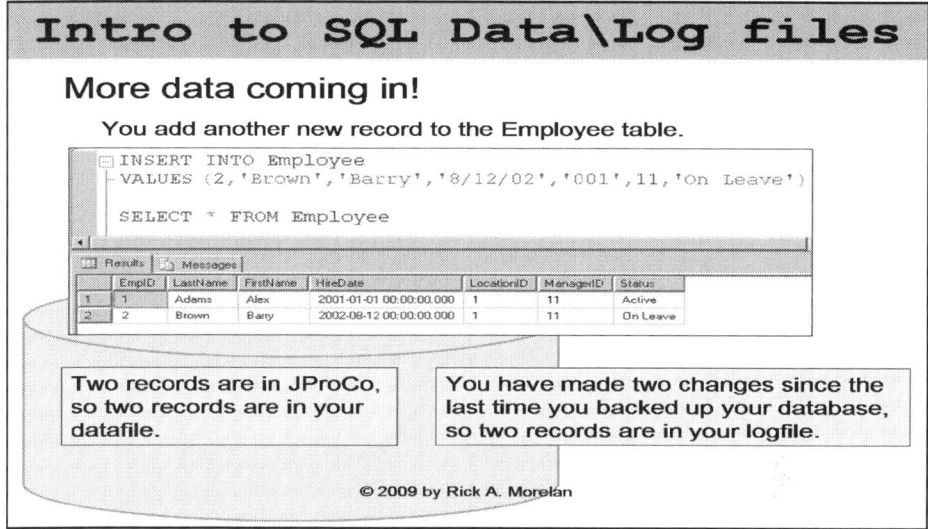

Figure 2.12 A total of two records are now in the database.

Step 4. The next step updates an existing record. Employee 2 is coming back from leave, so we are going to change his status from "On Leave" to "Active." There will still be two records in the database, so the datafile will contain two records. But there will be three records in the logfile, since we made three changes since the last time we backed up the database.

Chapter 2 Database File Structures

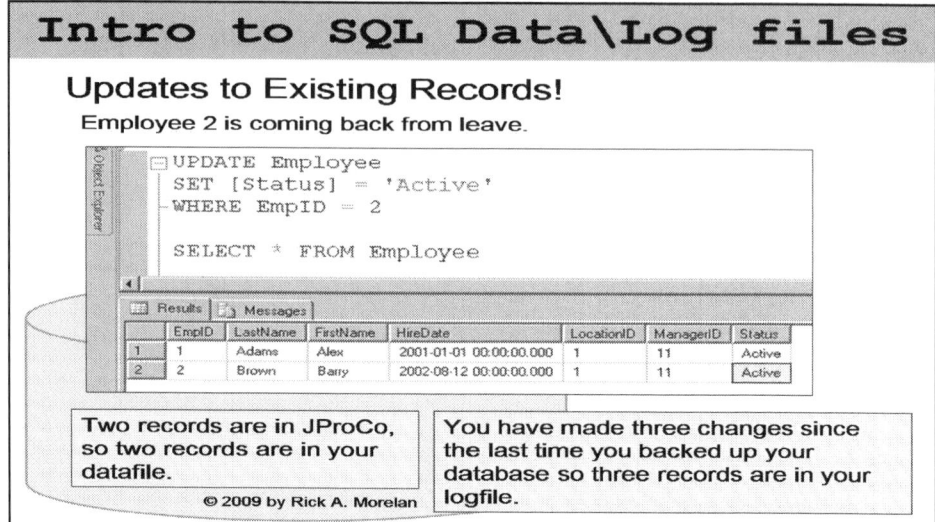

Figure 2.13 An existing record is updated; 2 records in the database but 3 records in the log.

Impact of the Database Backup Process

Step 5. The database is backed up nightly at midnight. After the three earlier changes happen, suppose it's after midnight and the database backup has just finished running. At 12:05AM, there would still be two records in the JProCo database, so we would have two records in the datafile. During most backup processes, the changes contained in the logfile are sent to the backup file. The logfile is truncated as part of the backup process, so zero records remain in the logfile immediately after each backup. How MSSQL handles this process will be discussed later – logfiles only issue checkpoints to flush the records upon log file backups. Regular backups do not impact the transaction log.

Chapter 2 Database File Structures

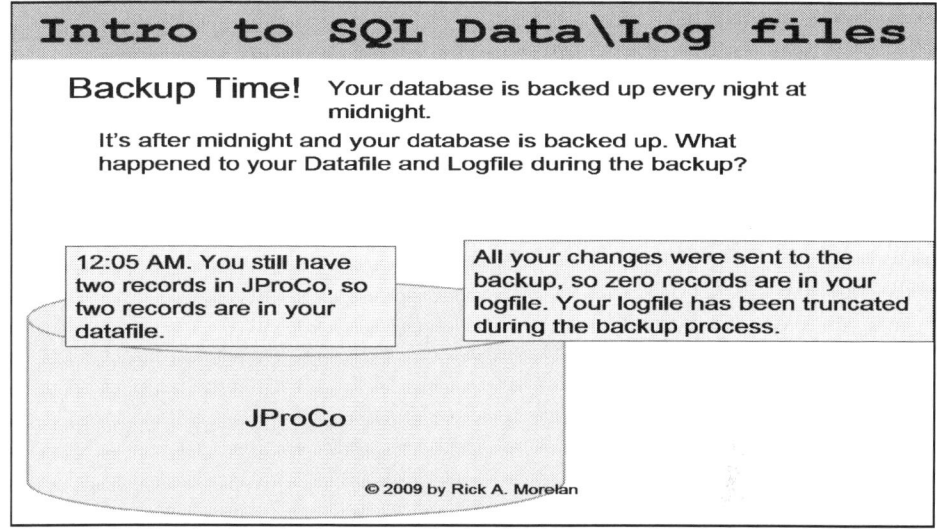

Figure 2.14 The database backup runs. The logfile is truncated, so it contains no records.

Step 6. On Day 2, we insert Lee Osako's record (the third record added to Employee). At this point we have three records in the datafile. The logfile has been emptied since the backup, and this change now adds one record to the logfile.

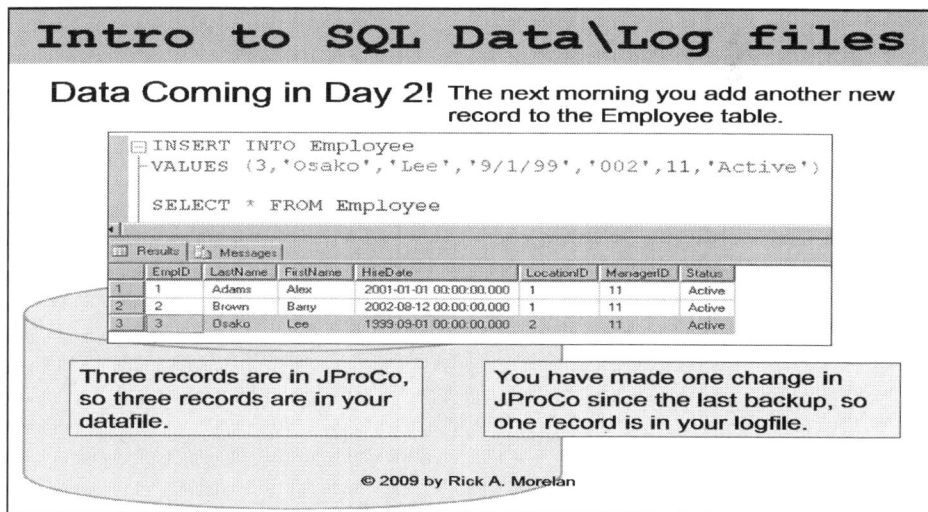

Figure 2.15 The third record is added to the db. Three records in database, one record in log.

Step 7. On the same day (Day 2), we delete Barry Brown from the table. Removing one record leaves two records in the datafile. The logfile now contains two records, one for the INSERT (Lee) and one for the DELETE (Barry).

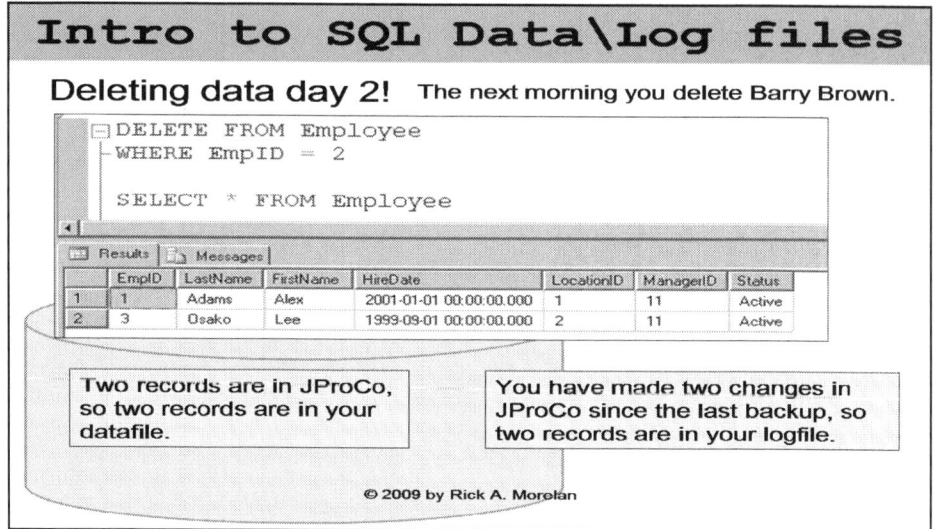

Figure 2.16 On Day 2 one record is deleted. Two records remain in MDF, two in LDF.

Recall Figure 2.16 where we saw the default data and log files which SQL Server originated when we created the JProCo database. It named the datafile JProCo.mdf and the logfile JProCo_log.ldf.

Chapter 2 Database File Structures

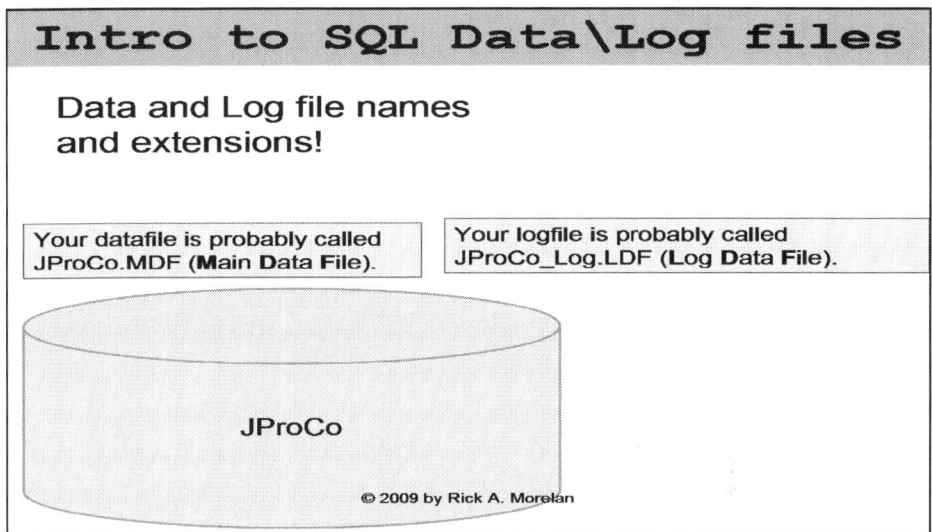

Figure 2.17 It is highly recommended that we follow the naming convention shown here.

This convention for naming files and the extensions reflect best practice recommendations. (Figure 2.17) *SQL Server does not enforce the .mdf/.ldf extensions, but following this standard is highly recommended.*

We know that SQL Server stores its data much like other applications – in files which are saved to a persistent drive. But a distinguishing feature of SQL Server is its robust ability to keep track of things over time. ***The security and safety of our data and reliability of the system are SQL Server's top priorities.*** Therefore, we can imagine that logging activity – which tracks every transaction made in the database – is a pretty big deal. Examples where logging saves the day generally involve some type of database restore or recovery need. Once a database backs itself up, we are generally assured a reliable mechanism we can use to restore the system in case something unfavorable happens. Suppose we notice bad data has come into our system through one of the periodic feeds. In fact, this data is so problematic that the team decides we must restore the database back to the point a week ago before the bad data began entering the system. *The periodic database backup is built using information provided by the logfile.* Logfiles keep track of the database transactions and help ensure data and system integrity, in case a system recovery is ever necessary.

Chapter 2 Database File Structures

Creating Databases

If we were to execute the statement in Figure 2.18, it would create a database called "TSQLTestDB," and all the defaults for name, size, and location of the datafile and logfile would be chosen by default. Up until now, we have accepted SQL Server's defaults for these items each time we have created a database.

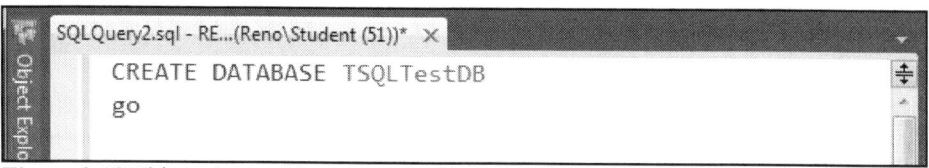

Figure 2.18 This code would create a db using defaults for name-size-location of MDF & LDF.

But we can actually choose our own options. For our examples in this chapter, we won't store any of our files in the default location. Create a folder titled SQL on the hard drive (C:\SQL). The MDF and LDF files for our new test database will be stored there.

In addition to specifying the location, we will also choose the name and size for TSQLTestDB's datafile and logfile. As a rule of thumb, it's generally a good idea to make the size of the LDF about 25% of the MDF. Now run all of this code together.

Chapter 2 Database File Structures

```
CREATE DATABASE TSQLTestDB
ON (NAME = TSQLTestDB,
FILENAME = 'C:\SQL\TSQLTestDB.mdf',
SIZE = 20MB)
LOG ON (NAME = TSQLTestDbLog,
FILENAME = 'C:\SQL\TSQLTestDB.ldf',
SIZE = 5MB)
```

Messages
Command(s) completed successfully.

Figure 2.19 We can choose the name, size, and location for the datafiles.

Let's check the C:\SQL folder and confirm we can see the newly created files TSQLTestDB.mdf (20 MB) and TSQLTestDB.ldf (5 MB).

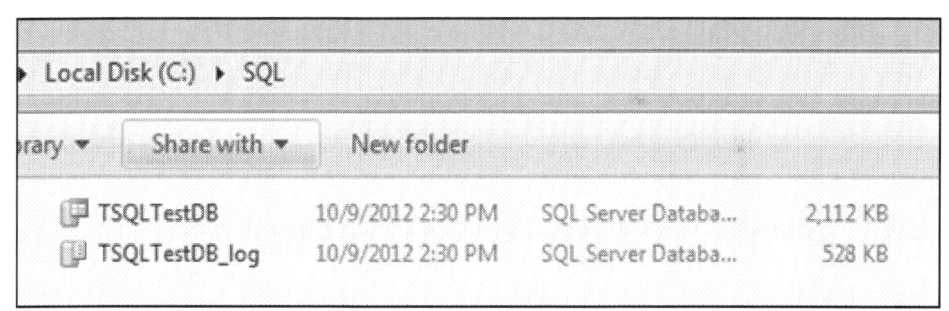

TSQLTestDB	10/9/2012 2:30 PM	SQL Server Databa...	2,112 KB
TSQLTestDB_log	10/9/2012 2:30 PM	SQL Server Databa...	528 KB

Figure 2.20 We specified the name, size, and location for TSQLTestDB, its MDF, and its LDF.

Now let's see how to locate metadata for this test database using SQL Server's Object Explorer. Remember to first refresh the Databases folder in the Object Explorer, since we know that SQL Server does not change its contents automatically (**Object Explorer** > right-click **Databases** > **Refresh**, as shown earlier in Figure 2.3).

Navigate to TSQLTestDB (**Object Explorer** > **Databases** > **TSQLTestDB**). Then open the Database Properties dialog by right-clicking the **TSQLTestDB** folder > **Properties**.

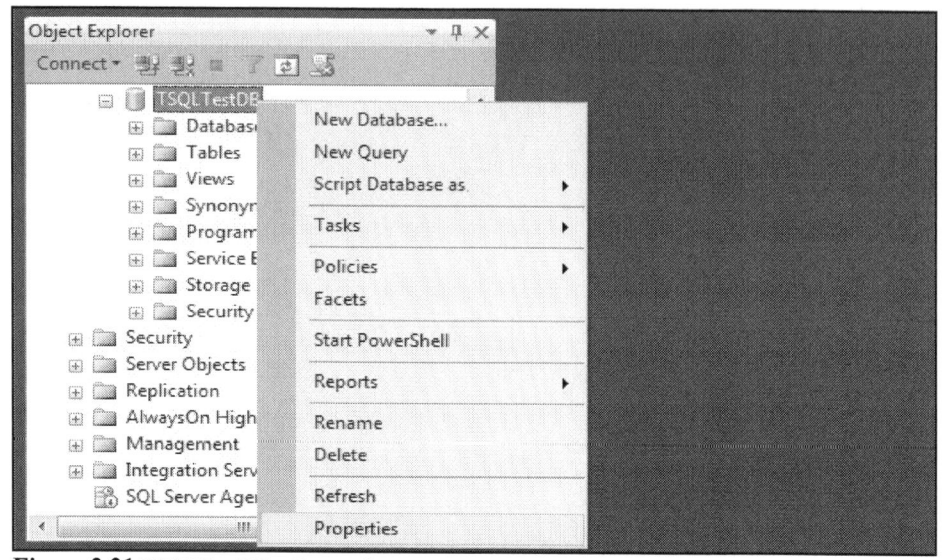

Figure 2.21 TSQLTestDB > Properties.

In the left-hand **Select a page** navigation menu, click the **Files** page. This will show the name for the database, the MDF, and the LDF. It shows the custom specifications included in the CREATE DATABASE statement

Chapter 2 Database File Structures

```
CREATE DATABASE TSQLTestDB
ON (NAME = TSQLTestDB,
FILENAME = 'C:\SQL\TSQLTestDB.mdf',
SIZE = 20MB)
LOG ON (NAME = TSQLTestDbLog,
FILENAME = 'C:\SQL\TSQLTestDB.ldf',
SIZE = 5MB)
```

Messages
Command(s) completed successfully.

Figure 2.22 The logical and physical name, size, and location (C:\SQL) for each file.

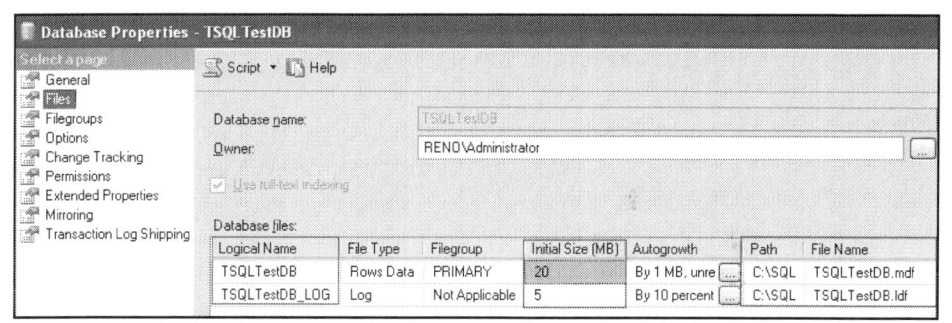

Logical Name	File Type	Filegroup	Initial Size (MB)	Autogrowth	Path	File Name
TSQLTestDB	Rows Data	PRIMARY	20	By 1 MB, unre...	C:\SQL	TSQLTestDB.mdf
TSQLTestDB_LOG	Log	Not Applicable	5	By 10 percent	C:\SQL	TSQLTestDB.ldf

Figure 2.23 The Database Properties dialog box shows metadata for the database TSQLTestDB.

Summary

The database is a direct reflection of all the data stored in the datafiles that make up the database. SQL allows us to choose where these datafiles are located. Databases change over time so the database is also changing. Datafiles often have the MDF or NDF extension. The datafiles cannot tell us what has changed a minute ago versus what has changed a year ago. The Log files keep track of what the latest changes are to the database. Log files continue to grow until they are truncated. If you backup your database then the log files are truncated at that time. Log files often have the LDF extension.

Points to Ponder
Database File Structures

1. Transact-SQL (T-SQL) statements are a common way to interact with SQL Server, view and modify data, or change the configuration of the server.

2. A new database can be built through the graphical UI (user interface) in SQL Server Management Studio or by using a CREATE DATABASE script.

3. Even when a graphical management tool is used to create or modify a database, the actions are translated into T-SQL statements and then executed.

4. SQL Server stores data in one or more datafiles.

5. A file is the physical allocation of space on disk. Each database has two or more files.

6. Datafiles hold the actual database objects and the data.

7. Regardless of how a database is created, T-SQL can be used to perform the following tasks:
    o Create and modify tables and indexes in a database.
    o Query objects by using the SELECT statement.
    o Insert and delete rows in a table.
    o Modify existing data in a table.
    o Repair a database.
    o Create a database.
    o Manage and connect to other databases.

Review Quiz – Chapter Two

1.) Which files get automatically truncated after a backup?

    O a. Datafile(s)
    O b. Logfile(s)

2.) What type of action will cause the logfile to grow but not the datafile?

    O a. SELECT
    O b. INSERT
    O c. UPDATE
    O d. TRUNCATE

3.) What type of action will cause the logfile and the data file to increase their size?

    O a. SELECT
    O b. INSERT
    O c. UPDATE
    O d. DELETE

Answer Key

1.) Datafiles hold all of the database data even after a backup so (a) is incorrect. After a backup the log file moves its data to the backup file and is truncated, making (b) the correct answer.

2.) The SELECT statement does not change the data so neither the datafile or the log file grows making (a) incorrect. INSERT will cause both the data and log files to grow making (b) incorrect. TRUCANTE does not affect the logfile. If we update a record the record could be the same size but each update is logged making (c) correct.

3.) If we insert a record that adds data to the database this action is also logged making (b) the correct answer.

Chapter 3. Full SQL Backup

It probably goes without saying that the smaller and faster nature of incremental backups and differential backups are only possible after a full backup has been made. This is because the very first incremental backup or differential backup looks to see what has changed since the last full backup. Therefore if there has never been a full backup then a differential or incremental backup cannot be done. Full backups are the key to any backup strategy. Since a full backup is all encompassing as previously mentioned in chapter 1, it includes everything needed in order to recover the database during the time the full backup is taken. It is also the foundation of any restore sequence.

Have you ever copied a file to a disk or USB drive? Most of the time we do this using Windows Explorer with a drag and drop operation. We may also be aware that we can use the command line utility (which looks like DOS) to copy that same file to your disk or USB drive. Either way we choose to do this, the same end results are our file was copied. Taking a full backup is one of the easiest tasks we can perform as a data professional. This can easily be performed within SSMS using the graphical UI or using T-SQL code. Regularly scheduled full backups should be a part of your organizations maintenance for production databases. Many say that this is the most important role as a database professional to ensure there are adequate backups on hand. In times of a disaster companies can rebuild applications, web, and database servers. On the other hand if they can't recover the data, it is nearly impossible to recreate it.

READER NOTE: *For the exercises in this chapter a folder needs to be created called Backups on the local C: drive (C:\Backups). Please run the script SQLBackupSetup01.sql in order to follow along with the examples for this chapter. All scripts mentioned in this chapter may be found in the "Solution Series" section at www.Joes2Pros.com.*

To make a full backup using the graphical UI within SSMS we need to follow a few simple steps. First right-click on the database and choose **Tasks** > and then select the **Back Up...** option. Do this now with JProCo. (Figure 3.1)

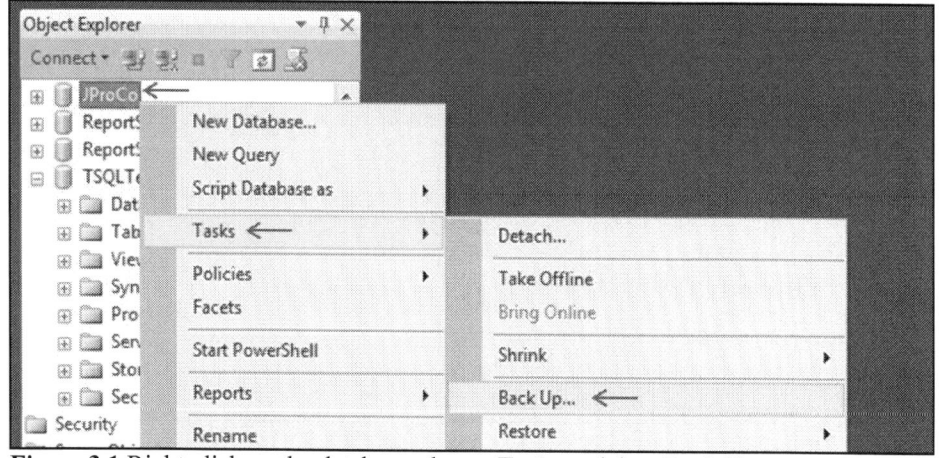

Figure 3.1 Right-click on the database, choose **Tasks** and then **Back Up...**

Once we have chosen **Back Up...**, the general dialog box appears where we can make a number of selections. If we were to select **OK** at this point, it will make a full backup of the database into the default backup location for the SQL Server instance. In Figure 3.2 the first option is to choose the database to backup. Next is the backup type we wish to make, in this case we want to choose **Full**. For **Backup component** we want to ensure **Database** is selected. Under **Backup set** we can specify the **Name** of the backup set. Typically we just accept the default value here. The next item is the destination and name of the backup file.

The default path is set at the instance level. For SQL 2012 the default location is the following Path:

C:\Program Files\Microsoft SQL Server\MSSQL11.MSSQLSERVER\MSSQL\Backup\

In our example we do not want to save in that location. To change this for this example select the path to highlight it and then click **Remove** > then click **Add** to make a new path.

Chapter 3 Full SQL Backup

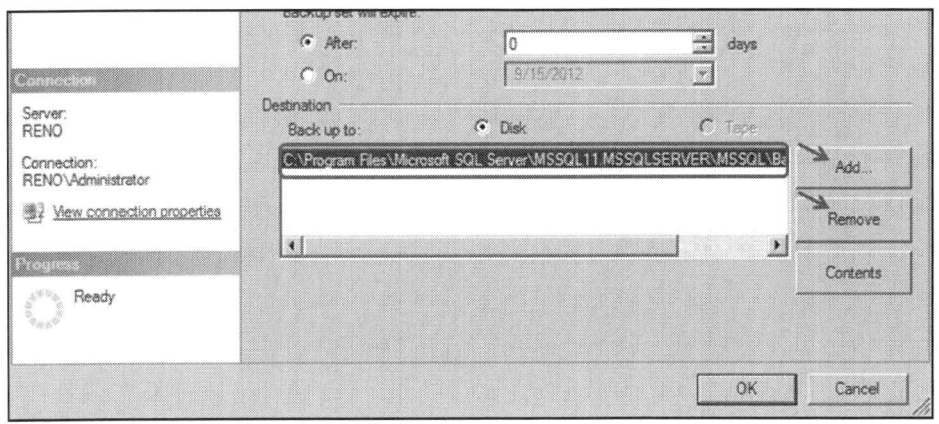

Figure 3.2 General options for backup.

To pick our own location, enter the path and name of the database backup file (Figure 3.3) to be created. A good best practice is to have a date and time included in the backup name as well as backup type. In this example change the backup file name to **JProCo_Full_MMDDYYYY.BAK**. Type the path and name of the database file. Replace MMDDYYYY with actual date value in the form of Month Day Year. For example, if today is May 16th 2013 then the filename should be JProCo_Full_05162013.BAK. This gives a nice visual aid rather than having to look at the timestamp on the file itself. Click **OK**.

READER NOTE: *When creating a custom backup job we would normally want to include HHMMSS in the name as well.*

Chapter 3 Full SQL Backup

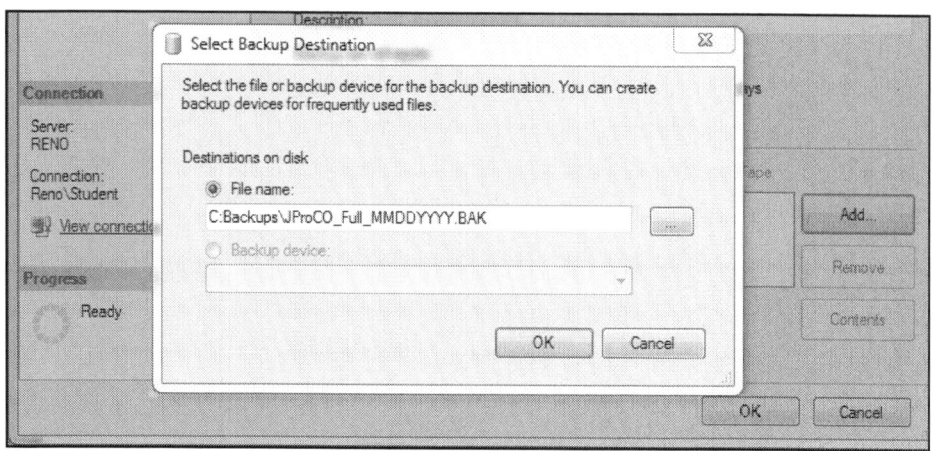

Figure 3.3 Type the path and name of the database file. Replace MMDDYYYY with actual date value in the form of Month Day Year.

Currently we have made many choices in the **General** page of the **Back Up a Database** window. Just below that click the **Options** page and to see that there are several more possible backup choices. Figure 3.4 shows the default values are already checked.

Odds are pretty good that anyone will perform many backups to the same database over time. If we backed up the database 10 times does that mean we have 10 backup files or can we put 10 backups into 1 big file? The answer is we get to choose. If we append backups and use the same filename each time, then that one filename will hold many backup sets. Be careful not to use the same name each time or it might overwrite the old backup and only have the latest backup saved.

Overwrite media defaults to **Append to the existing backup set**. This was chosen to maintain backup history by putting many backup sets into one backup file. If we chose to make multiple backups and use the same file name each time, there would be multiple backup sets within that single backup file. If we want to overwrite the old backup with the latest backup of the same name we will have to select the **Overwrite all existing backup sets** option.

Why is it a good idea to have a spare key to your car? I bought a new car six months ago and had a spare key made. On a very important day I found the spare should have been tested. The key did not work and my original key was lost. After a very expensive house call from the locksmith to re-create the data of my key, I learned to test my backup key and not just assume it will work.

The next section is called Reliability. A false sense of security may come with choosing some of the reliability options. The recommended option is to "**Verify backup when finished**" however that does not mean the backup file is 100% valid. The only true way to fully verify a backup is to restore it. Everyone should have a process in place to regularly test backups by performing restores.

Anyone who has ever packed for a long trip has discovered that compressing their clothes into on suitcase by reducing the amount of space they take up allows them to pack more items in the limited space. By reducing the amount of wasted space in their suitcase they are more efficient at carrying more items, therefore reducing the need to carry an additional bag. SQL Server (depending on the version) can also utilize compression. Backing up using compression means that (in most cases) our backups will take up much less space and also take less time to complete due to requiring less device I/O.

If we are using a version of SQL Server that supports compression we will see that option listed. We can use one of the three options:

- o Use the default server setting
- o Compress backup
- o Do not compress backup

We will use the default option. Click **OK** and the JProCo database will backup to: C:\Backups\JProCo_Full_MMDDYYYY.BAK.

Chapter 3 Full SQL Backup

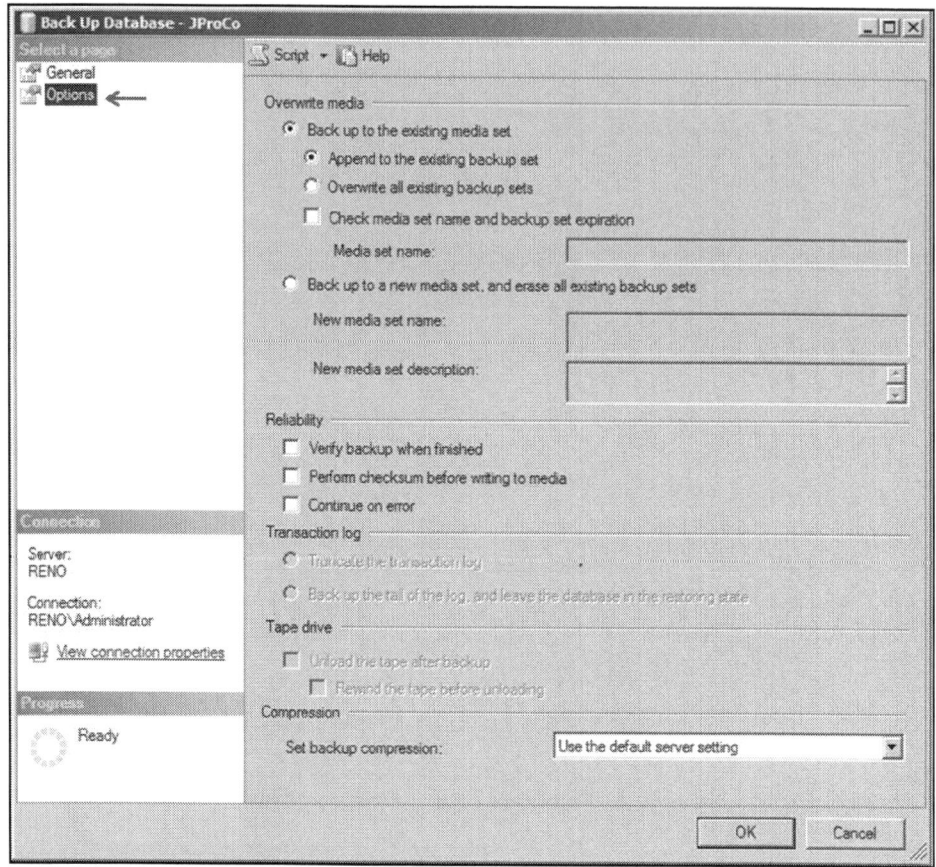

Figure 3.4 Additional options for backups.

Using T-SQL

There are many choices and options for making a backup. If we clicked all the right buttons and did everything perfectly then we will likely be asked to do it again many times. By forgetting one checkbox just one time, it can cause the wrong type of backup which could be unusable or worse yet, accidently overwrite a file we many need later. If these perfect set of steps could be laid out into a T-SQL script then we just need to run that script at the right time. This way the chance for human error is significantly reduced. Therefore the preferred choice for making backups is to use T-SQL code.

The syntax to backup with T-SQL code is very straightforward:

BACKUP DATABASE DB_NAME TO <backup_device> WITH <options>

In our example let's name our backup so it's easy to tell that T-SQL was used to create this file. To do this we will also append _TSQL in the file name. This is different from the file name we created using the graphical UI in the last section. Type the path and name of the database file. Replace MMDDYYYY with actual date value in the form of Month Day Year. For example, if today is May 16th 2013 then the filename should be JProCo_Full_05162013.BAK

Let's go ahead and make a full backup by using the following script:

```
BACKUP DATABASE JProCo TO DISK =
'C:\Backups\JProCo_FULL_MMDDYYYY_TSQL.BAK'
```

Messages
Command(s) completed successfully
0 rows

Figure 3.5 Shows full backup was successful.

When using the graphical UI, there were lots of options to choose from such as append, overwrite, verify backup, and many more. When using T-SQL many of these options are also available by using the WITH clause.

One handy feature of a graphical UI restore is that a display box shows us the percentage of the database that has been restored. To show the percentage restored using T-SQL code we will need to use WITH STATS = X (with X being the increment of percentage). So WITH STATS = 10 the restore process would display percentages from 0, 10, 20 …100 as it completes. Most DBAs use a 1 or 10 as percentage increments.

To use compression we would use WITH COMPRESSION in the syntax. If we wish to overwrite the existing backup file we would use WITH INIT in the syntax.

Restoring Using the Graphical UI

Restoring using the graphical UI is much like backing up the database using the graphical UI. In Figure 3.6 we start this by right clicking the database (like JProCo) and choose **Tasks** > **Restore** > **Database**.

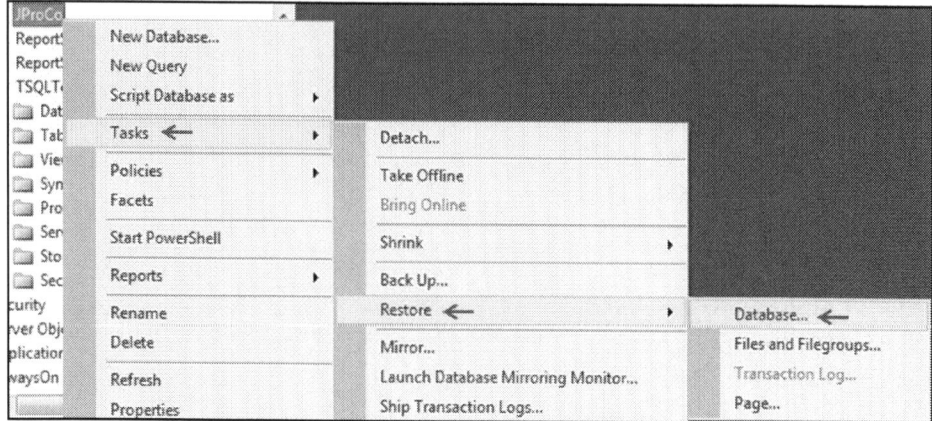

Figure 3.6 Right-click on the database, chose **Tasks** > **Restore** > **Database**.

A new window will open on the **General** page prompting the choice of the database source and destination. We can restore from the backup files we have or even restore from a live database to another without taking a backup. Since we typically restore database files from one server to another (such as production to a test server) we will choose **Device** as our **Source** and then click the ellipsis. (Figure 3.7)

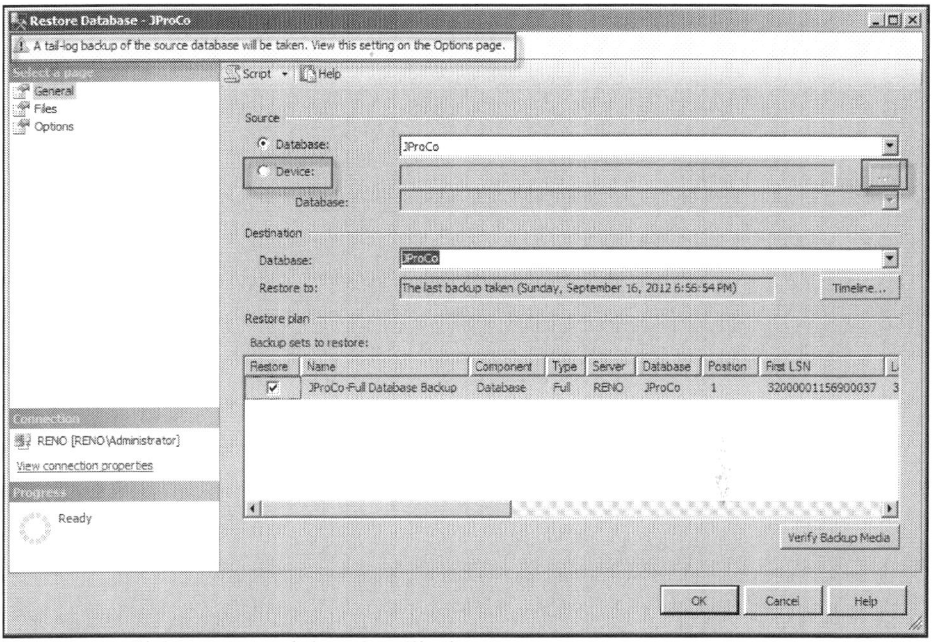

Figure 3.7 Click **Device** and then the ellipsis.

Where is that backup file located? SQL will want to know this and here is the chance to tell it exactly where that file was saved. We need to select our backup file to restore our database and add that exact path to SQL Server. In Figure 3.8 our Backup media type should be file and then click **Add**.

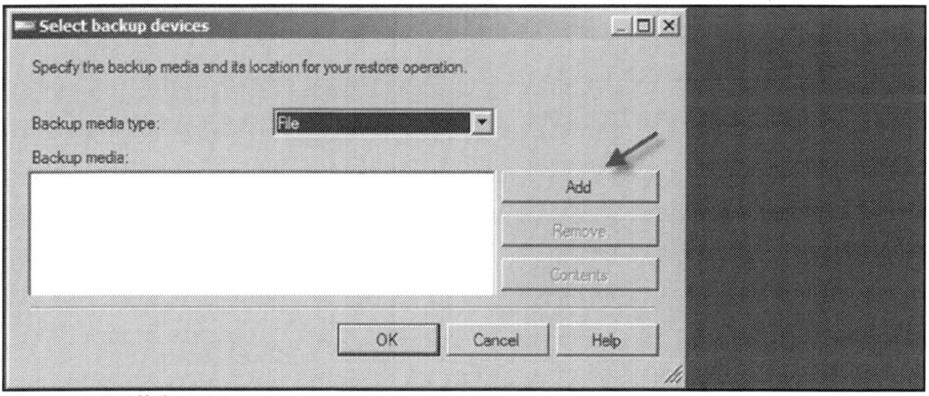

Figure 3.8 Click **Add**.

Chapter 3 Full SQL Backup

Our file was saved to the C drive in the backup folder. So for this demo just browse to the C: \Backups folder to see both files that were created. We can then select either backup file since they are the same. Select the first one and chose **OK**. (Figure 3.9)

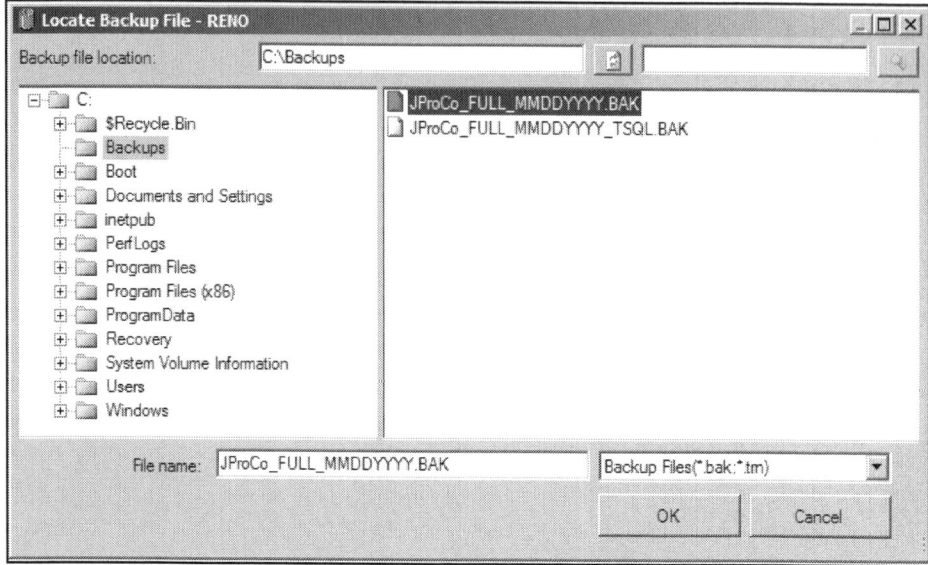

Figure 3.9 Browse to C:\Backups, select the file and click **OK**.

This returns us back to the general page of **Restore Database** window. Click on the **Files** page to see that we can change the location of where to restore the data and log file. In some situations we may have to restore a database to a server that does not have the exact same disk configuration. We also may want to restore the files to a location other than the default location for that instance. (Figure 3.10)

Chapter 3 Full SQL Backup

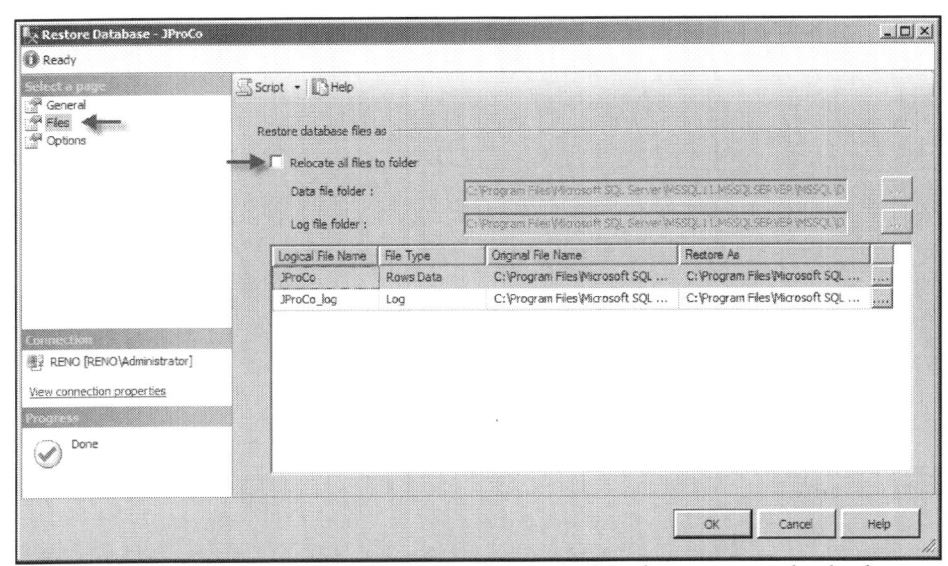

Figure 3.10 The **Files** page is where we can change the location to restore the database files.

Now click on the **Options** page. (Figure 3.11) On this page we have a number of restore options to choose from. Check the box to **Overwrite the existing database (WITH REPLACE)**.

Some restores will come from the full backup and other times there will be a need to restore a differential afterwards. So know ahead of time is this all of our data or do we have some differential backups to do to add in more data? In our example we only took this full backup and no other types of backups. Since this is the only restore we are going to do before making the database live, the **Recovery state** should be set to **RESTORE WITH RECOVERY**. By choosing to restore with recovery we are setting the database to be open and running as soon as this restore is completed.

As we will see in future chapters sometimes we will need to leave the database offline so that additional restores can be applied. Next make sure the box to **Take tail-log backup before restore** is unchecked. This particular option in the restore dialog is new to SQL Server 2012. We will be covering tail-log backup terminology in Chapter 5.

Chapter 3 Full SQL Backup

Nobody should be connected to or using this database until we are done with the restore. There might be some system connections that should be told to disconnect during this restore. We can close any existing connections to the database by checking the box **Close existing connections to destination database**.

READER NOTE: *I typically like to check for existing connections using the SP_WHO2 system stored procedure to ensure I am not affecting any active users.*

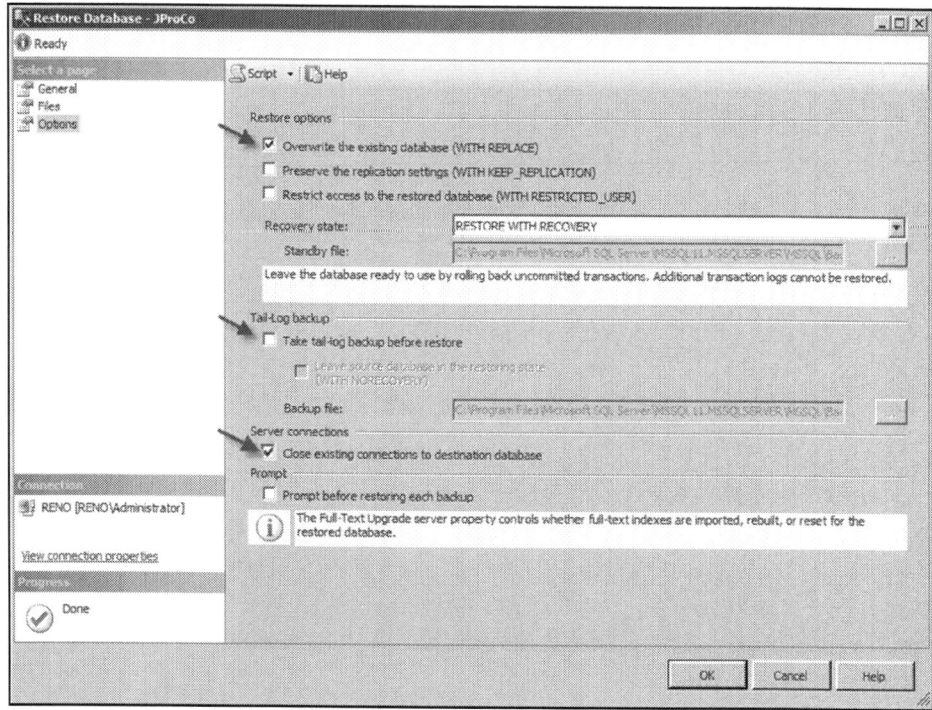

Figure 3.11 Check to Overwrite and uncheck the box to backup the tail-log.

We are now ready to restore the database so click **OK**. Congratulations, with this process we have successfully restored the JProCo database. (Figure 3.12)

Figure 3.12 Confirmation window that the database was restored.

Restoring Using T-SQL

The true benefit to using T-SQL code is once we get it right we can run the code anytime. If we use the point and click method we need to make our choices each time we run the backup. This makes T-SQL the preferred choice for performing restores. This also allows us to keep a generic script saved that has all the syntax we usually use so that we don't have to retype it each time we need to restore a database. All we have to do is make a few changes for that particular restore and execute the script.

The syntax for a database restore using T-SQL is RESTORE DATABASE DB_NAME FROM <backup_device> WITH <options>. There are several options that we can use after the WITH statement. We can specify the recovery setting RECOVERY / NORECOVERY / STANDBY. In this case we will be fully recovering the database so users can connect by specifying RECOVERY.

We can also use WITH MOVE to specify the location of the database files, or REPLACE to overwrite the existing database. As stated earlier there is also the choice to see the progression of the restore by using STATS. Type the path and name of the database file. Replace MMDDYYYY with actual date value in the form of Month Day Year. For example, if our backup was created on May 16th 2013 then the filename could be 'C:\Backups\JProCo_Full_05162013.BAK':

```
USE [MASTER]
RESTORE DATABASE [JProCo]
FROM DISK = 'C:\Backups\JProCo_Full_MMDDYYYY.BAK'
WITH MOVE 'JProCo'
TO 'C:\Program Files\Microsoft SQL Server\
    MSSQL11.MSSQLSERVER\MSSQL\DATA\JProCo.mdf',
MOVE 'JProCo_log'
TO 'C:\Program Files\Microsoft SQL Server\
    MSSQL11.MSSQLSERVER\MSSQL\DATA\JProCo_log.ldf',
STATS = 1, REPLACE
```

READER NOTE: *The code above is a likely location for the JProCo MDF and LDF file(s). We can always get the properties of JProCo and select the **files** page to see where the database storage is located.*

Summary

Full backups are the key to any backup strategy. Full backups include everything needed in order to recover the database. We can easily make and restore full backups using the graphical UI or using T-SQL. Having a regularly scheduled full backup is critical to protecting our organizations' data assets. This can easily be accomplished either using the built in database maintenance plan or creating our own custom SQL Agent job. The only way to fully validate that our backups are good is to regularly restore them.

Points to Ponder - Full Backup

1. Full backups contain the entire database including all files and file groups associated with the database.
2. A full database backup provides a complete copy of the database.
3. Backups do not cause blocking contrary to any myths out there; however backups are very I/O intensive which can cause performance issues related to I/O if they are run during high peak times.

4. DBCC CHECKDB should be run routinely on the databases. Databases can become corrupt for various reasons and SQL Server will happily backup those corrupt pages. In order to find the corruption, we must run CHECKDB regularly.

Review Quiz – Chapter Three

1.) A full backup consists of which items?

   O a. All transactions since the last full backup.
   O b. Only changed data since the last full backup not resetting the flag.
   O c. Everything needed to fully recover the database.
   O d. Only the primary file group.

2.) When restoring a database, which recovery setting should be used to recover the database leaving it in a usable state?

   O a. NORECOVERY
   O b. STANDBY
   O c. ONLINE
   O d. RECOVERY

3.) When restoring a database using T-SQL, which command would be used to over write the existing database?

   O a. WITH OVERWRITE
   O b. WITH REPLACE
   O c. WITH FORCE
   O d. WITH COMMIT

Answer Key

1.) A full backup contains all data needed to fully recover the database. This would include all file groups and enough portion of the transaction log needed. Therefore answer (c) is correct.

2.) To restore the database and set it for online connections to connect we need to "recover" the database. Answer (d) is correct.

3.) When choosing to overwrite an existing database during a restore using T-SQL, we must use the WITH REPLACE command. Using the graphical UI we would select the box to overwrite the existing database. Answer (b) is correct.

Chapter 4.   Differential SQL Backups

When we clean our kitchens after dinner and wash the dishes, we don't empty our cabinets and wash every dish in our kitchen. We simply wash the dishes that we have dirtied. When backing up data, if we only want to backup the data that has changed we can make a differential backup as we covered in Chapter 2. Differential backups backup all the changed data since the last full backup. A differential backup does not reset the differential bitmaps (or bitmap marker) indicating it has been backed up. Implementing a backup strategy that utilizes full and differential backups can drastically reduce our backup time and space required to store historical backups. In some cases it has been reported that switching to a weekly full and daily differential backup made a difference of backing up 2.5 TB weekly to less than 2 GB. Consider how much of the database is static data that doesn't change. If we are performing daily full backups, we are backing up the same unchanged data every single night.

The advantage to taking full backups every night is the restore strategy is easy. Just grab the latest backup. Implementing a backup strategy using full and differential backups also alters the restore strategy. It adds an additional step for the restore process. We must first restore the full backup with NORECOVERY so that we can then restore the differential backup with RECOVERY. Since most differential backups are small, the additional time to restore them is usually done in minutes. This slight increase in restore time is usually an acceptable trade off for the decrease in amount of disk space required for backups. Most experiences have proven that the additional step to restore a differential backup has only added minutes to the restore time and it still fits well within service level agreements.

READER NOTE: *For the exercises in this chapter a folder needs to be created called Backups on the local C: drive (C:\Backups). Please run the script SQLBackupSetup01.sql in order to follow along with the examples for this chapter. All scripts mentioned in this chapter may be found in the "Solution Series" section at www.Joes2Pros.com..*

Chapter 4 Differential SQL Backups

Since differential backups can only be made after a full backup, let's reuse our full backup script from Chapter 3. Type the path and name of the database file. Replace MMDDYYYY with actual date value in the form of Month Day Year. For example, if the backup was made on May 16th 2013 then the filename could be 'C:\Backups\JProCo_Full_05162013.BAK':

```
BACKUP DATABASE JProCo TO DISK =
'C:\Backups\JProCo_FULL_MMDDYYYY_TSQL.BAK'
```

Using the Graphical UI

To make a differential backup using the graphical UI within SSMS we need to follow a few simple steps just like we did for the full backup. First, right-click on the database we want to backup and choose **Tasks** > and the **Back Up...** option. Do this now with JProCo. (Figure 4.1)

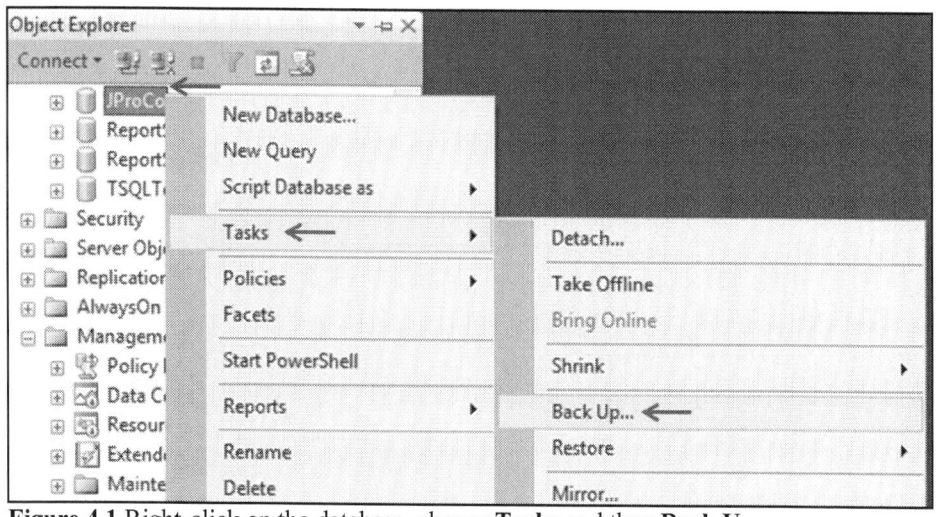

Figure 4.1 Right-click on the database, choose **Tasks** and then **Back Up...**

Once we have chosen **Back Up...**, the general dialog box appears where we can make a number of selections. In Figure 4.2 the first option is to choose the database we want to backup. Next is the backup type we wish to make, in this case we want differential. For **Backup component**: we want to ensure **Database** is selected and under **Backup set** we can specify

Chapter 4 Differential SQL Backups

the **Name** of the backup set. Typically we would just accept the default value for **Name** of the **Backup set**. The next item is the **Destination** and the name of the backup file it listed under **Back up to**. The default path is set at the instance level. For SQL 2012 the default location is:

C:\Program Files\Microsoft SQL Server\MSSQL11.MSSQLSERVER\MSSQL\Backup\. We want to change the path so for this example, click **Remove** and then click **Add**.

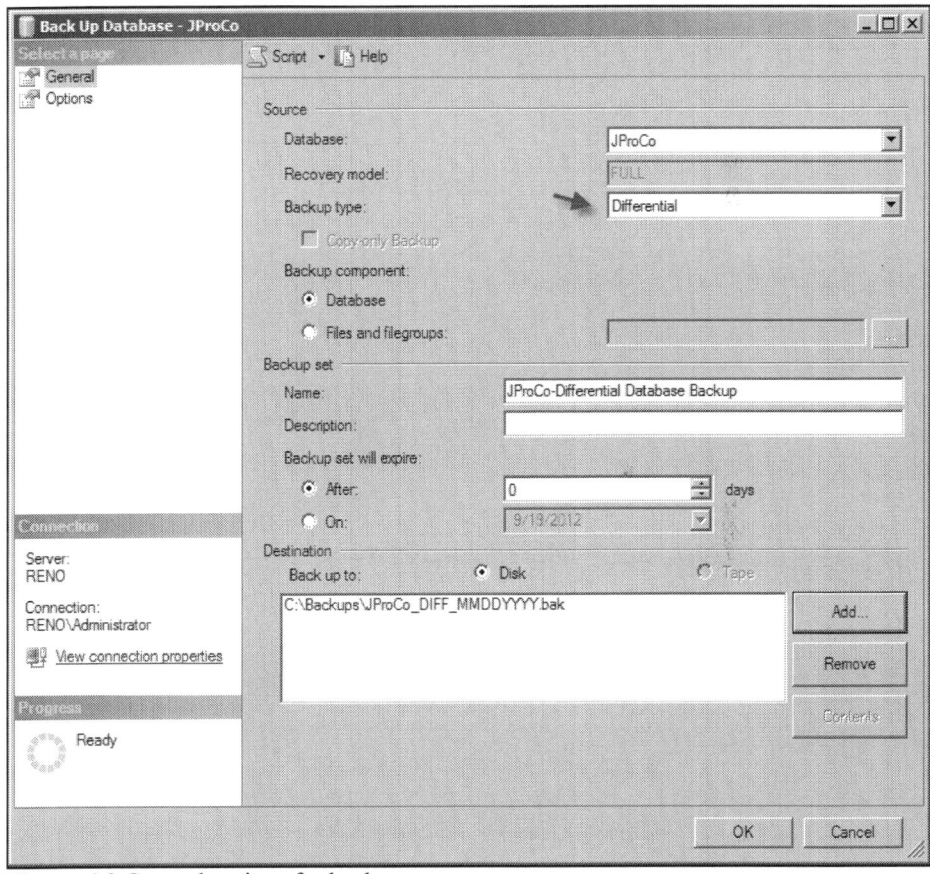

Figure 4.2 General options for backup.

Type the path and name of the database backup file. (Figure 4.3) As with full backups, best practice is to have a date and time included in the backup name as well as the backup type. Type the path and name of the

61

www.TimRadney.com
wwwJoes2Pros.com

Chapter 4 Differential SQL Backups

database file. Type the path and name of the database file. Replace MMDDYYYY with actual date value in the form of Month Day Year. For example, if today is May 16th 2013 then the filename should be JProCo_DIFF_05162013.BAK. This gives a nice visual aid rather than having to look at the timestamp on the file itself. Now click **OK**.

When creating a custom backup job we would want to include HHMMSS in the name as well.

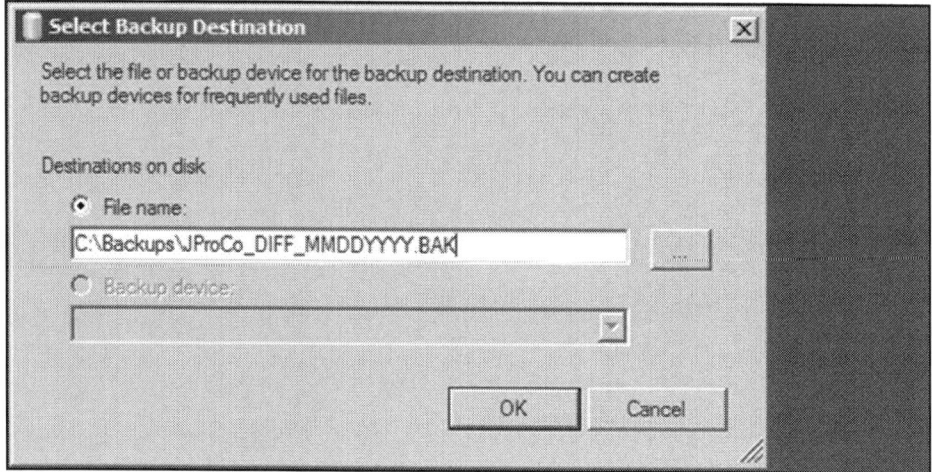

Figure 4.3 Type the path and name of the database file. Replace MMDDYYYY with actual date value in the form of Month Day Year.

Click **Options** page to see that we have several more options as we did in Chapter 3 on full backups. In Figure 4.4 we will see the default values. The **Overwrite media** option defaults to **Append to the existing backup set**.

Just like with full backups, differential backups must be verified by restoring them regularly. It is still recommend to **Verify backup when finished** however that does not mean the backup file is 100% valid. If our backup solution includes full and differential backups, the restore validation should also include restoring from full and differential backups.

Compression is also an option with differential backups and performs the same way as it does with full backups. We will use the default option here as we did in the previous chapter. Click **OK** and the JProCo database will backup to **C:\Backups\JProCo_DIFF_MMDDYYYY.BAK**.

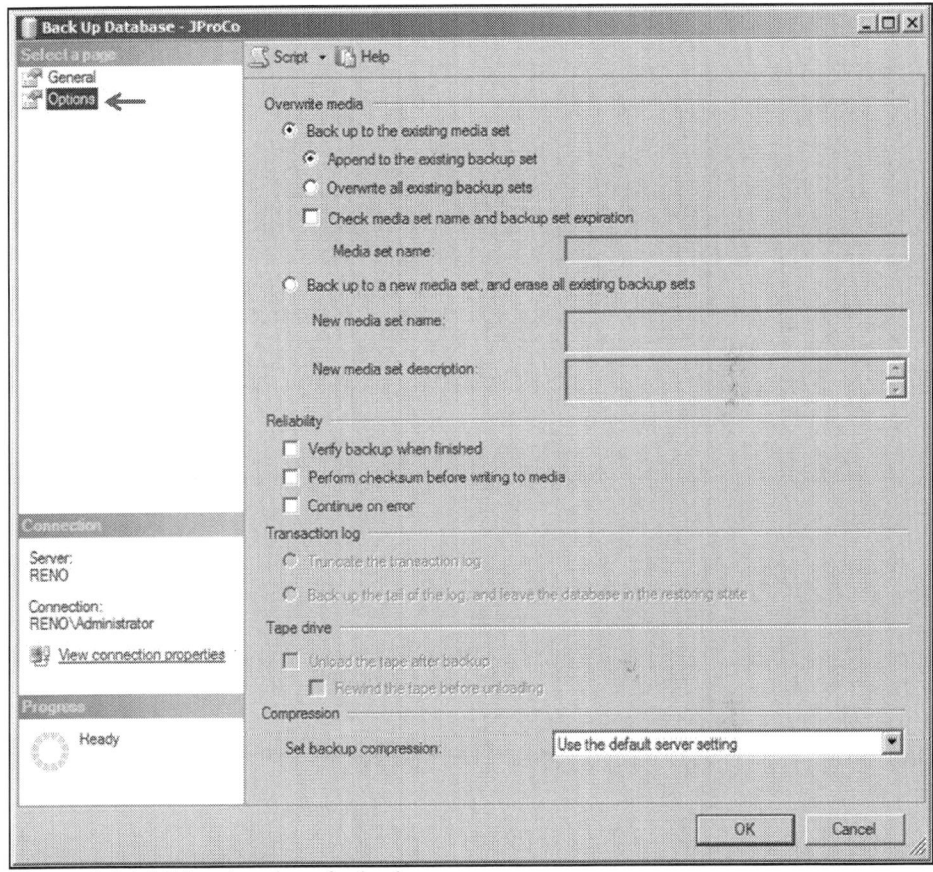

Figure 4.4 Additional options for backups.

Using T-SQL

We covered the benefits of using T-SQL in Chapter 3 explaining how having to check so many boxes each time we do a backup can be cumbersome. One can also state that anything worth repeating should be scripted. Backups are certainly worth repeating, therefore we should script them out for easier and more consistent reproduction. For that reason, the preferred choice for making backups is to use T-SQL.

The syntax is very straightforward. We specify:

BACKUP DATABASE DB_NAME TO <backup_device> WITH <options>

and then specify our options. Since we are making a differential backup we have to specify WITH DIFFERENTIAL. To name this file differently than we did in the UI example let's mark this backup file name. Let's include _TSQL in the file name and both backup files we created. This way we have the backup files used from the UI along with the new ones we're creating now. We want all backup files from this chapter to be present.

Type the path and name of the database file. Type the path and name of the database file. Replace MMDDYYYY with actual date value in the form of Month Day Year. For example if the backup was made on May 16th 2013 then the filename could be 'C:\Backups\JProCo_DIFF_05162013.BAK':

```
BACKUP DATABASE JProCo TO DISK =
  'C:\Backups\JProCo_DIFF_MMDDYYYY_TSQL.BAK'
WITH DIFFERENTIAL
```

Restoring Using the Graphical UI

Using the graphical UI to restore a differential backup is exactly like it is to restore a full backup. As a matter of fact, our first step is to restore the full backup as we did in Chapter 3.

In order to restore a differential database, we must first restore the prior full backup that the differential belongs to. We will need to follow the steps in Chapter 3, however in the graphical UI we would specify the equivalent **RESTORE WITH NORECOVERY** on the options page. Fortunately when restoring multiple files (such as our full and differential backup) we can chain them together using the graphical UI. Let's get started by right-clicking the database and choose **Tasks** > **Restore** > **Database**. (Figure 4.5)

Chapter 4 Differential SQL Backups

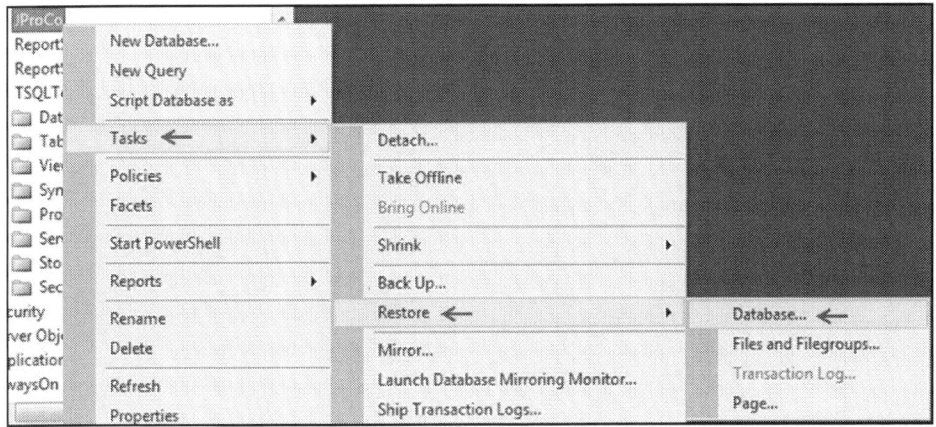

Figure 4.5 Right-click on the database, chose **Tasks** > **Restore** > **Database**.

A new window will open on the **General** page prompting the choice of the database source and destination. We can restore from the backup files we have or even restore from a live database to another without taking a backup. Since we typically restore database files from one server to another (such as production to a test server) we will choose **Device** as our **Source** and then click the ellipsis. (Figure 4.6)

Chapter 4 Differential SQL Backups

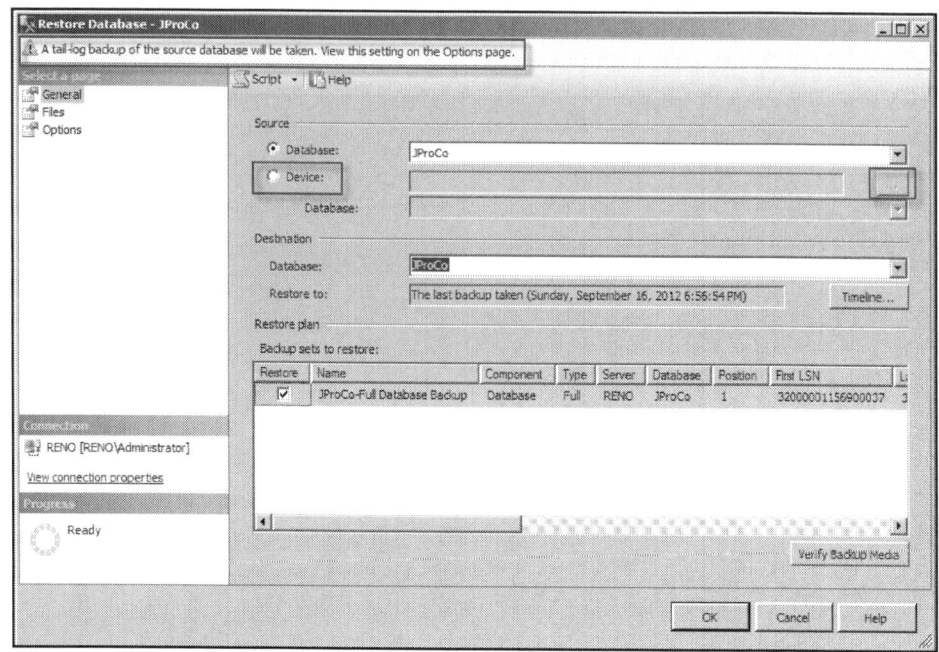

Figure 4.6 Click **Device** and then the ellipsis.

Where are those backup files located? SQL will want to know this and here is the chance to tell it exactly where those files are saved. We need to select our backup file to restore our database and add that exact path to SQL server. In Figure 4.7 our Backup media type should be **Files** and then click **Add**.

Figure 4.7 Click **Add**.

66

www.TimRadney.com
www.Joes2Pros.com

Chapter 4 Differential SQL Backups

Our file was saved to the C drive in the backup folder. For this demo just browse to the C: \Backups folder to see our backup files that we created. We can then select our full backup file and the differential that belongs to the full. Chose **OK** and then **OK** once more. (Figure 4.8)

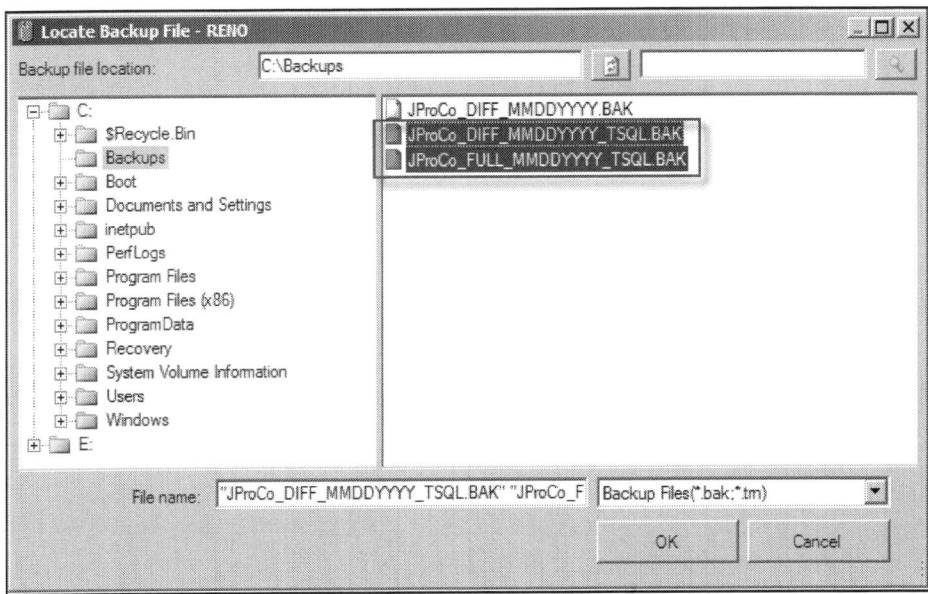

Figure 4.8 Browse to C:\Backups, select the files and click **OK**.

This returns us back to the **Restore Database** window. Click on the **Files** page to see that we can change the location of where to restore the data and log file. In some situations we may have to restore a database to a server that does not have the exact same disk configuration. We also may want to restore the files to a location other than the default location for that instance. (Figure 4.9)

Chapter 4 Differential SQL Backups

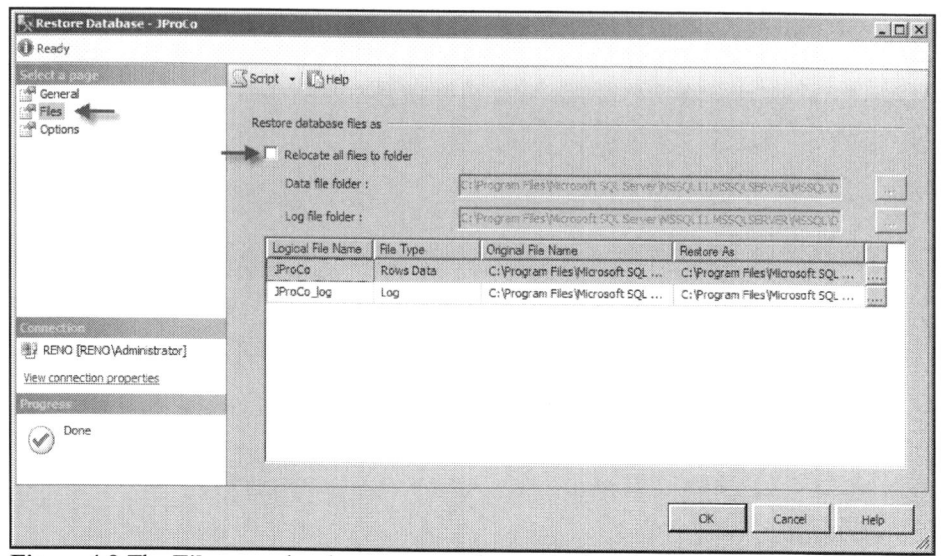

Figure 4.9 The **Files** page is where you can change the location to restore the database files.

Now click on the **Options** page. (Figure 4.10) On this page we have a number of restore options to choose from. Check the box to **Overwrite the existing database** (**WITH REPLACE**).

This is where we could leave the database offline so that additional restores can be applied or bring the database online. Next to "Recovery state", choose the option that states "RESTORE WITH RECOVERY" since we will not be restoring any additional files. Next uncheck the box to **Take tail-log backup before restore**. This particular option in the restore dialog is new to SQL Server 2012. We will be covering tail-log backup terminology in Chapter 5.

Nobody should be connected to or using this database until we are done with the restore. There might be some system connections that should be told to disconnect during this restore. We can close any existing connections to the database by checking the box **Close existing connections to destination database**.

Chapter 4 Differential SQL Backups

READER NOTE: *I typically like to check for existing connections using SP_WHO2 system stored procedure to ensure I am not affecting any active users.*

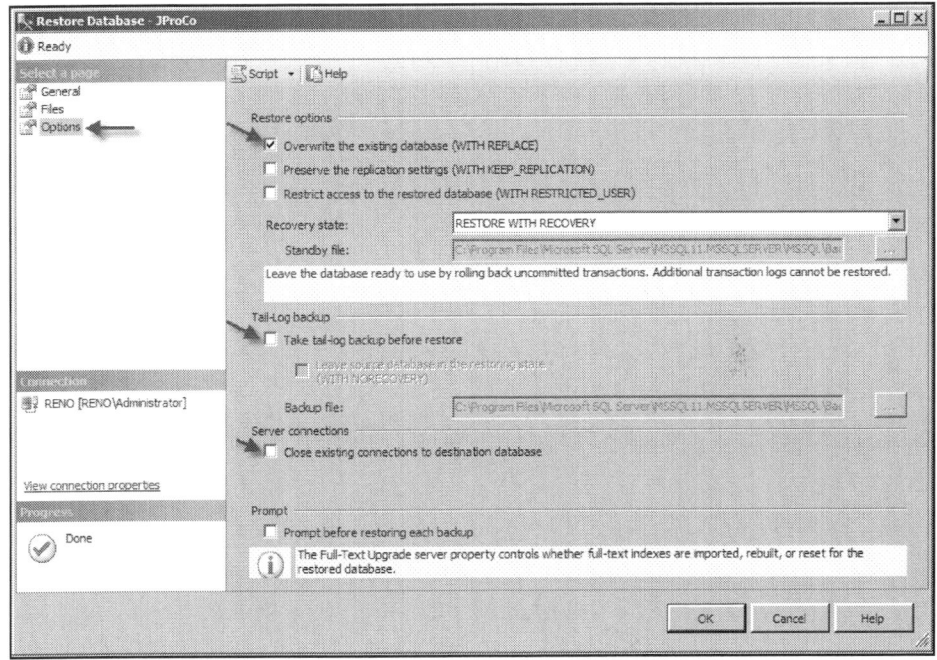

Figure 4.10 Restore Database Options Page.

We are now ready to restore the JProCo database full and differential backups. Click **OK**. (Figure 4.11)

Figure 4.11 Confirmation window showing that the restore ran.

Chapter 4 Differential SQL Backups

Restoring Using T-SQL

Just like with our restore script from Chapter 3 the preferred choice for performing restores is to use T-SQL. Once we get our T-SQL script right, we can save the script for future use. Anytime that we need to perform another full and differential restore we can access our saved script, make whatever changes are needed, and execute the code.

Just like we did in the graphical UI step, we have to restore the full backup that belongs to the differential database backup before we can restore the differential.

The syntax for a database restore using T-SQL is RESTORE DATABASE DB_NAME FROM <backup_device> WITH <options>. There are several options that we can use after the WITH statement. We can specify the recovery setting RECOVERY / NORECOVERY / STANDBY. In our case we need to restore our full database with NORECOVERY, and then we will restore our differential with RECOVERY to bring the database online. Since the default of a restore is WITH RECOVERY, technically we do not have to specify it during the differential restore. We can also use WITH MOVE to specify the location of the database files. We can use REPLACE to overwrite the existing database. We can use STATS to monitor the progression of the restore. Type the path and name of the database file. Replace MMDDYYYY with actual date value in the form of Month Day Year. For example, if today is May 16th 2013 then the filename for the full should be JProCo_Full_05162013.BAK. This gives a nice visual aid rather than having to look at the timestamp on the file itself:

```
USE [MASTER]
GO
RESTORE DATABASE [JProCo]
FROM DISK = 'C:\Backups\JProCo_Full_MMDDYYYY.BAK'
WITH MOVE 'JProCo'
TO 'C:\Program Files\Microsoft SQL Server\
  MSSQL11.MSSQLSERVER\MSSQL\DATA\JProCo.mdf',
MOVE 'JProCo_log'
TO 'C:\Program Files\Microsoft SQL Server\
```

```
  MSSQL11.MSSQLSERVER\MSSQL\DATA\JProCo_log.ldf',
STATS = 1, REPLACE , NORECOVERY

USE [MASTER]
GO
RESTORE DATABASE [JProCo]
FROM DISK = 'C:\Backups\JProCo_DIFF_MMDDYYYY_TSQL.BAK'
WITH MOVE 'JProCo'
TO 'C:\Program Files\Microsoft SQL Server\
  MSSQL11.MSSQLSERVER\MSSQL\DATA\JProCo.mdf',
MOVE 'JProCo_log'
TO 'C:\Program Files\Microsoft SQL Server\
  MSSQL11.MSSQLSERVER\MSSQL\DATA\JProCo_log.ldf',
STATS = 1, REPLACE
```

Summary

Adding differential backups into the backup routine can significantly reduce the overall backup time and reduce the backup storage requirements. Each differential backup will back up all changed data since the last full backup. A backup routine of weekly full and daily differentials will see the daily differential grow each day since each new daily backup would contain all the changes since the last full backup. Using a backup routine of full and differentials will require a change to the restore routine as well. We will have to restore the full backup first with NORECOVERY before applying the differential backup.

Points to Ponder
Differential Backup

1. A differential backup runs like a full backup, but only contains the data that has changed since the last full backup.

2. Differential backups are a great mechanism to help move or migrate a database. For example, if at 10:00 PM we need to backup 500GB of databases and restore to a new server, then at 8:00 PM we could make

a full backup, copy it to the new server and restore with NORECOVERY, then at 10:00 PM make a differential to capture the changed data and copy and restore it.

3. Differential backups cannot be restored by themselves; we must restore the previous full backup.

4. Just like full backups, differential backups can cause additional I/O, so caution should be taken making differential backups during peak times, if there has been a considerable amount of data change since the last full backup.

Review Quiz – Chapter Four

1.) A differential backup consists of which items?
- O a. All transactions since the last full backup.
- O b. Only changed data since the last full backup not resetting the flag.
- O c. Everything needed to fully recover the database.
- O d. Only the primary file group.

2.) When recovering a differential database, we have to restore the previous full database with NORECOVERY first.
- O a. TRUE
- O b. FALSE

3.) When restoring the full database prior to restoring the differential, which recovery setting should be used to recover the full database?
- O a. NORECOVERY
- O b. STANDBY
- O c. ONLINE
- O d. RECOVERY

Answer Key

1.) A differential backup contains all changed data since the last full backup and does not reset the flag/marker when backed up. Therefore answer (b) is correct.

2.) To restore a differential backup, we must restore the full backup associated with the differential first. When restoring the full backup, the database must be left in a non-recovered state so we can restore the differential. Answer (a) is correct

3.) To restore a differential backup, we must restore the full backup associated with the differential first. When restoring the full backup, the database must be left in a non-recovered state so we can restore the differential. Answer (a) is correct.

Chapter 5. Transaction Log Backups

In today's modern age it is more and more common for every household to use a digital video recorder (DVR) with the TV. One of the benefits of having a DVR is allowing the viewer to be able to rewind or replay something they just watched. Think of the transaction log of our database as a recorder. We discussed in Chapter 2 that the transaction log is part of the database file structure. The transaction log is a key part of the database due to it maintaining the records for all the database modifications.

In the video recorder example did you know that a movie is actually 60 still pictures flashing in sequence to give it the look of real motion? There are 60 frames per second so in a 20 second commercial there are 1,200 frames. The video editors might speak to each other in terms of which ordered frame(s) to edit for the finished work. For example in the 20 second commercial they might say let's start to fade to a blur dream effect between frames 810 and 825. The higher the frames number the further into the video we are.

SQL Server is a motion of data instead of pictures and it too markets its steps much like frames in a movie. Each data modification is uniquely identified with a log sequence number (LSN), which are ordered. An LSN, which is higher in number, occurred after an LSN with a lower number. The LSNs are very important during restores to track the order of events as well as the point in time in which data has been restored.

If the transaction log held every record from the database and every change made to the database then it would be even larger than all the data files combined. This could make the database slow and storage cost too expensive. The transaction log should be relatively small and nimble. For this reason regular maintenance of the transaction log is critical or else the transaction log will grow until the server runs out of disk space. To maintain the transaction log and to free up the stored transactions within it, we need to regularly truncate the log. When we truncated the log we don't want to lose this data. The best way to do this is by backing up the transaction log. This is like moving the data from the transaction log into a small backup file. Not only does backing up the log help manage the size, it also decreases the overall vulnerability for data loss.

Someone is likely paying us to keep his or her system healthy and safe. The expectations on how well they expect us to keep things running are called a Service Level Agreement (SLA). The agreement might be that we can't allow more than 1 hour of data loss. Depending on the SLA the scheduled transaction log backups should meet or exceed the agreement. If the organization states that a system cannot sustain more than 30 minutes of potential data loss, then the scheduled transaction log backups should occur at an interval at least every 30 minutes.

The process of backing up and restoring transaction logs is very similar to that of differential backups. In order to restore a transaction log backup, we must first restore the full backup, and then differential if they are part of the backup routine, then we can start applying the transaction logs in order.

Regular transaction log backups should be part of the regular backup routine for any database in full recovery model.

READER NOTE: *For the exercises in this chapter a folder needs to be created called Backups on the local C: drive (C:\Backups). Please run the script SQLBackupSetup01.sql in order to follow along with the examples for this chapter. All scripts mentioned in this chapter may be found in the "Solution Series" section at www.Joes2Pros.com.*

Chapter 5 Transaction Log Backups

In order to be able to make transaction log backups, the recovery model of the database must be one that supports logging transactions. These two recovery models are full and bulk_logged. We can check the recovery model of the database by right-clicking on the database, choosing **Properties**, and then clicking on the **Options** page. (Figure 5.1) In our example we are using the JProCo database which is in the full recovery model. If our JProCo database had been using a recovery model that did not support transaction log backups we could change it here to **Full** or **Bulk_logged**.

To begin making transaction log backups after changing to **Full** or **Bulk_logged** recovery model, first make a full backup. Click **OK**.

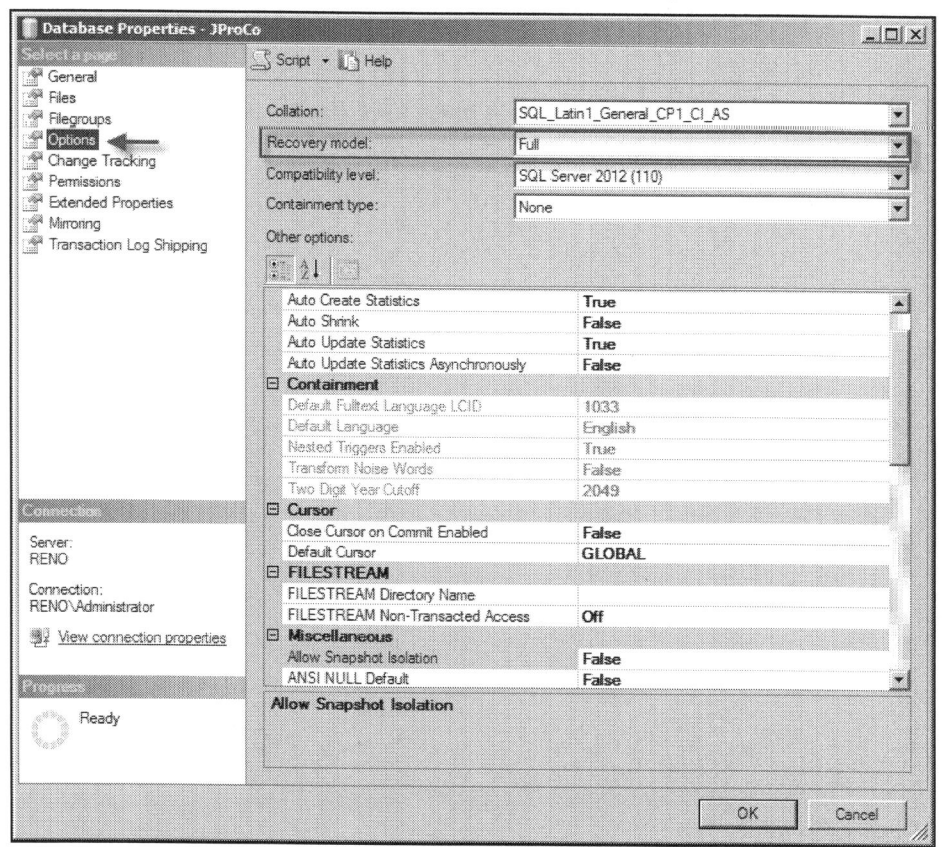

Figure 5.1 In the **Options** page of **Database Properties** we can view the recovery model.

Chapter 5 Transaction Log Backups

It is very likely that we will sometime come across a database where a transaction log backup cannot be done due to the recovery model not supporting it. When trying to backup the transaction log using T-SQL the error will be similar to the message below:

```
Messages
Msg 4208, Level 16, State 1, Line 1
The statement BACKUP LOG is not allowed while the recovery model is
SIMPLE. Use BACKUP DATABASE or change the recovery model using ALTER
DATABASE.
Msg 3013, Level 16, State 1, Line 1
BACKUP LOG is terminating abnormally.

                                                                    0 rows
```

If we are using the graphical UI to make a backup, then **Transaction Log** will not be listed. If we are trying to restore a transaction log to a database that is in a recovery model that does not support them, then **Transaction Log** will be greyed out as shown in Figure 5.2.

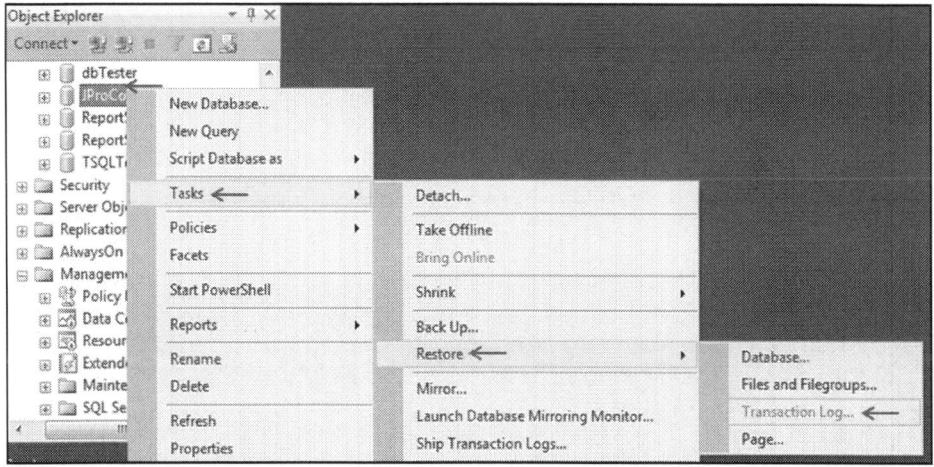

Figure 5.2 If the database is not in the correct recovery model or a full backup has not been taken after switching to a supported recovery model then **Transaction Log** restore option is not listed.

Since we did the steps of Figure 5.1 we are ready to get started on our backups. Since transaction log backups can only be made after a full

77

Chapter 5 Transaction Log Backups

backup, let's reuse our full backup script from Chapter 3. Execute the following script to get started:

```
BACKUP DATABASE JProCo TO DISK =
'C:\Backups\JProCo_FULL_MMDDYYYY_TSQL.BAK'
```

Using the Graphical UI

By now we should be very familiar with the graphical UI to make backups. To make a transaction log backup using the graphical UI within SSMS we need to follow a few simple steps just like we did for the full and differential backups. First right-click on the database we want to backup and choose **Tasks** > and then the **Back Up...** option. Do this now with JProCo. Figure 5.3

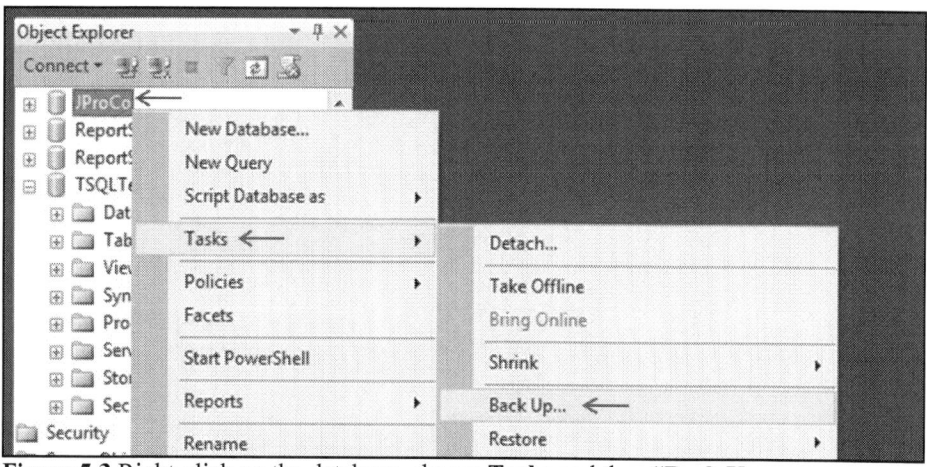

Figure 5.3 Right-click on the database, choose **Tasks** and then "Back Up...

Once we have chosen **Back Up...** , the **General** page of the **Back Up Database – JProCo** window box appears where a number of selections can be made. In Figure 5.2 the first option is to choose the database we want to backup. Next is the backup type we wish to make, in this case we want transaction log. For **Backup set** we can specify the **Name**, which typically we would just accept the default value here. The next item is the destination and name of the backup file. The default path is set at the instance level. For SQL 2012 the default location is:

C:\Program Files\Microsoft SQL Server\MSSQL11.MSSQLSERVER\MSSQL\Backup\.

For this example we want to replace that value so click **Remove** > **Add**.

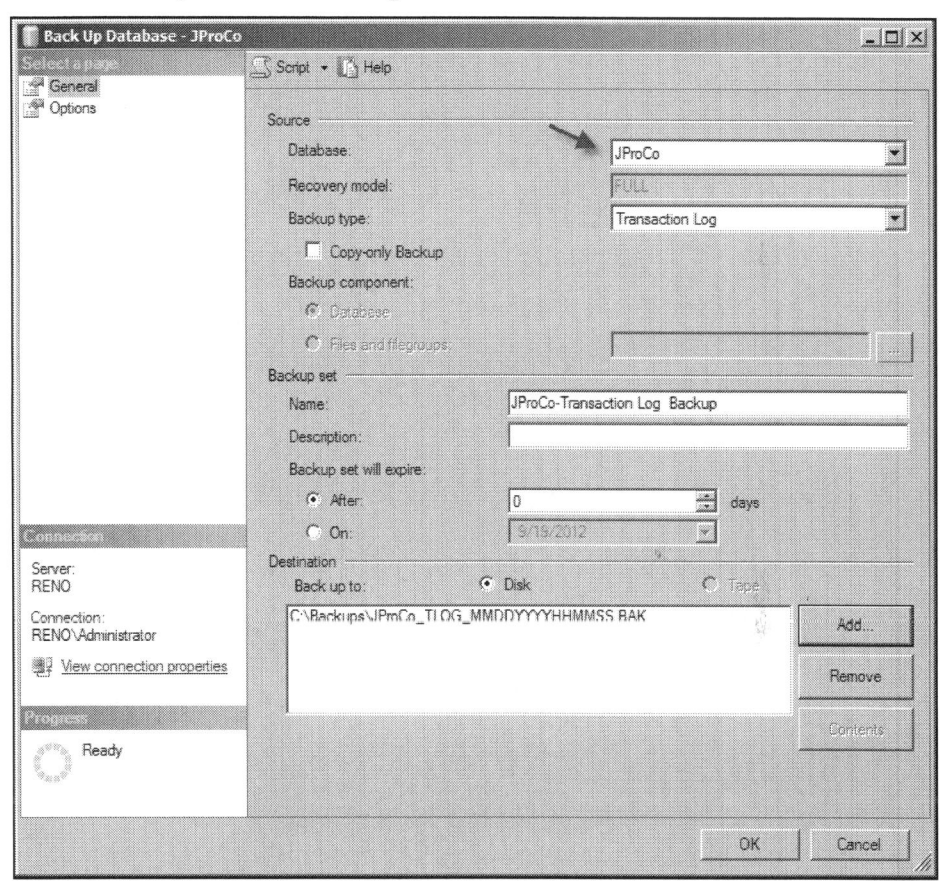

Figure 5.4 General options for backup.

Type the path and name of the database backup file. (Figure 5.5) No different than with full and differential backups, the best practice is to have the date and time included in the backup name in addition to the backup type. This is even more important with transaction log backups since we typically make more than one of them per day. All transaction

Chapter 5 Transaction Log Backups

log backups should have a unique file name. Type the path and name of the database file. Replace MMDDYYYY with actual date value in the form of Month Day Year. For example if today is May 16th 2013 at 10:05.30 AM then the filename should be
JProCo_TLOG_05162013100530.BAK Click **OK**.

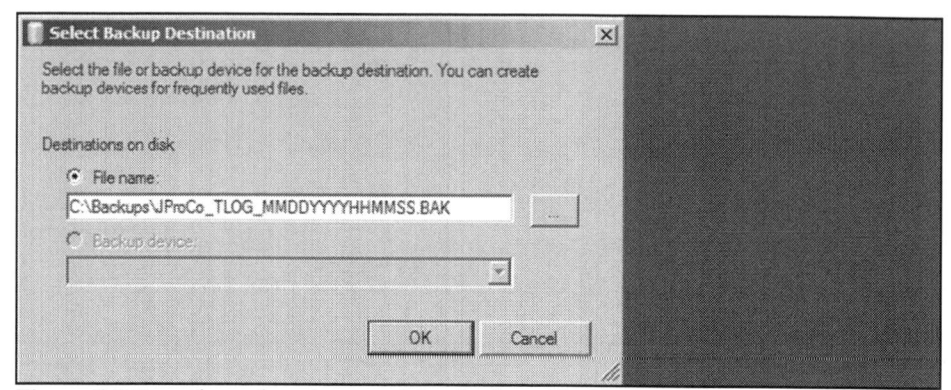

Figure 5.5 Type the path and name of the database file. Replace **MMDDYYYYHHMMSS** with actual date value in the form of Month Day Year Hour Minute Seconds.

Click the **Options** page to see that there a several more options as we did in the previous two chapters. In Figure 5.6 we will see the default values. **Overwrite media** defaults to **Append to the existing backup set**. Just like with full and differential backups, transaction log backups must be verified by restoring them regularly. It is still recommend to "**Verify backup when finished**" however that does not mean the backup file is 100% valid. If our backup solution includes making transaction log backups, then they should also be part of the restore validation checks that we perform. By regularly restoring the full backups and applying transaction logs to them, we are testing the backup solution and getting excellent experience by performing disaster recovery tests.

If we are responsible for being able to fully recover the database environment and we are not familiar with recovering a database server up to a point in time, then practice and practice often. We have a new section listed for **Transaction log**. In this section we can choose to truncate the transaction log or backup the tail of the log, and leave the database in the

Chapter 5 Transaction Log Backups

restoring state. The default here is to truncate the transaction log, which will free up log space. The option to back up the tail log will back up the active log and is used in preparation to restore the database. If we choose this option the database will become unavailable to all the users. Ensure that **Truncate the transaction log** is selected. Compression is also an option with transaction log backups and performs the same way as it does with full and differential backups. We will use the default option here as we did in the previous chapter. Click **OK** and the JProCo database will backup to:

C:\Backups\JProCo_TLOG_MMDDYYYYHHMMSS.BAK.

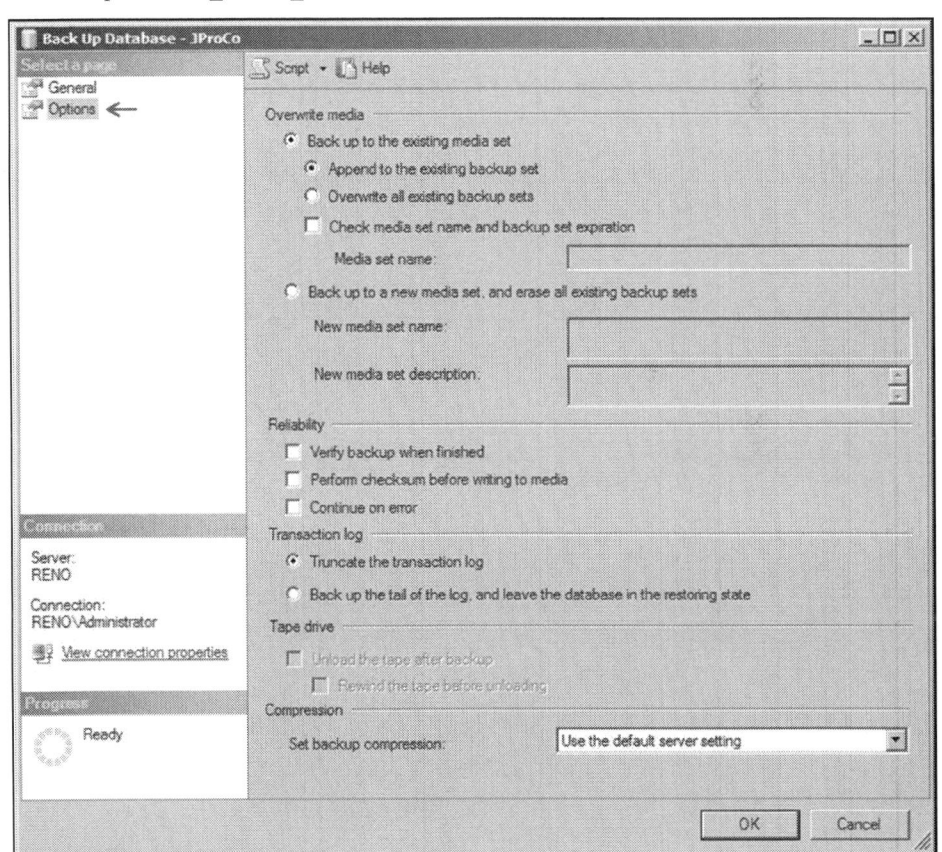

Figure 5.6 Additional options for backups.

READER NOTE: *If the log backup fails it's likely because your full backup did not complete first.*

Using T-SQL

If using T-SQL was a benefit for making full or differential backups, it is certainly beneficial for transaction log backups as well. Transaction log backups are made multiple times per day, in most cases several times per hour. Using T-SQL is the preferred choice for making transaction log backups.

In this example we should insert a new record so that we can capture it in our transaction log. Let's begin by confirming that we do not have a contractor by the name of Muhammad Wong in our contractor's table by executing the following script:

```
SELECT LastName, FirstName
FROM JProCo.[dbo].[Contractor]
WHERE LastName = 'Wong' AND FirstName = 'Muhammad'
```

This should get a received "(0 row(s) affected)". Now let's insert a record to add Muhammad Wong as a contractor by executing the following script:

```
INSERT INTO JProCo.[dbo].[Contractor]
([LastName], [FirstName], [hiredate], [LocationID])
VALUES
('Wong', 'Muhammad', '2012-04-18', '1')
```

The syntax for backing up a transaction log is very similar to other backups. Just specify the BACKUP LOG DB_NAME TO <backup_device> WITH <options> syntax. Let's include _TSQL in the file name to not append to the file we created using the graphical UI. Let's execute the following code:

```
BACKUP LOG JProCo TO DISK = 'C:\Backups\
  JProCo_TLOG_MMDDYYYYHHMMSS_TSQL.BAK'
```

Restoring Using the Graphical UI

Differential backups are only possible if you have taken a full backup first. The full backup acts as the base backup for differential backups and sometimes as the base for log file backups. In order to restore transaction logs to our database, we must first restore the prior full backup that the transaction logs belong to. If we were also making differential backups then we would first restore the full backup, then the most recent differential as the base for the transaction backup. After the most recent full and differential are restored as your base then you can restore the transaction logs (in order) since that last differential backup.

To get started we will need to follow the steps in Chapter 3, however we will need to specify **WITH NORECOVERY** in the T-SQL script for the full backup. In the graphical UI we would specify the equivalent **RESTORE WITH NORECOVERY** on the **Options** page. Fortunately when restoring multiple files, such as full, differential, and or transaction log backups we can chain them together using the graphical UI. Let's get started by right-clicking the database and choosing **Tasks** > **Restore** > **Database**. (Figure 5.7)

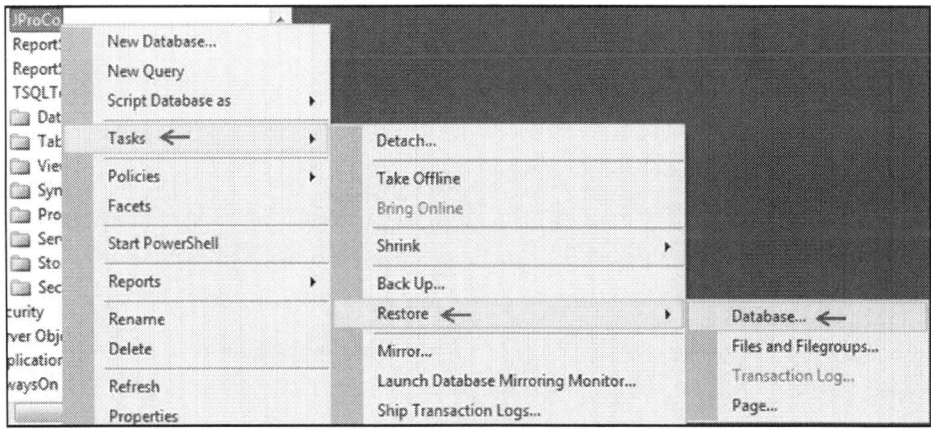

Figure 5.7 Right-click on the database, chose **Tasks** > **Restore** > **Database**.

Chapter 5 Transaction Log Backups

A new window will open on the **General** page prompting the choice of the database source and destination. We will choose **Device** as our **Source** and then click the ellipsis. (Figure 5.8)

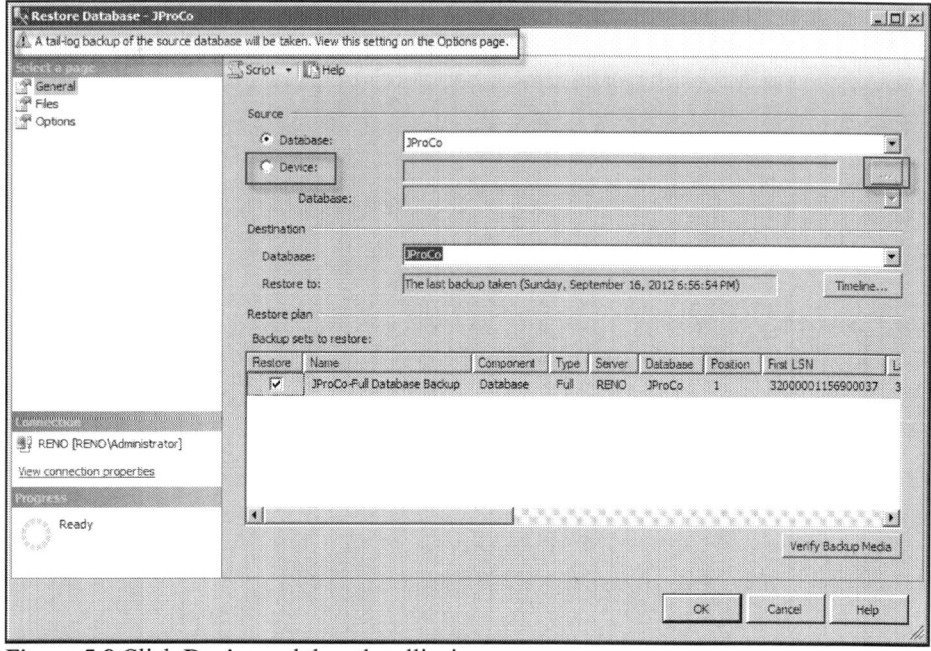

Figure 5.8 Click **Device** and then the ellipsis.

Where are those backup files located? SQL will want to know this and here is the chance to tell it exactly where those files are saved. We need to select our backup files to restore our database and add that exact path to SQL Server. In Figure 5.9 our Backup media type should be **File** and then click **Add**.

Chapter 5 Transaction Log Backups

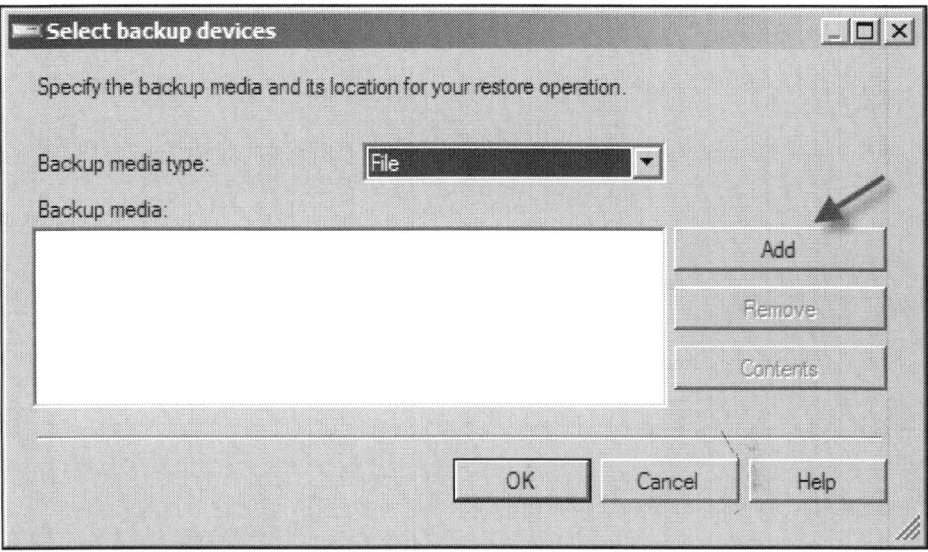

Figure 5.9 Click **Add**.

Our files were saved to the C drive in the backup folder. For this demo just browse to the C: \Backups folder to see our backup files that we created. We can then select our full backup file and our transaction log backups that belong to the full backup. Chose **OK** and then **OK** once more. (Figure 5.10)

Chapter 5 Transaction Log Backups

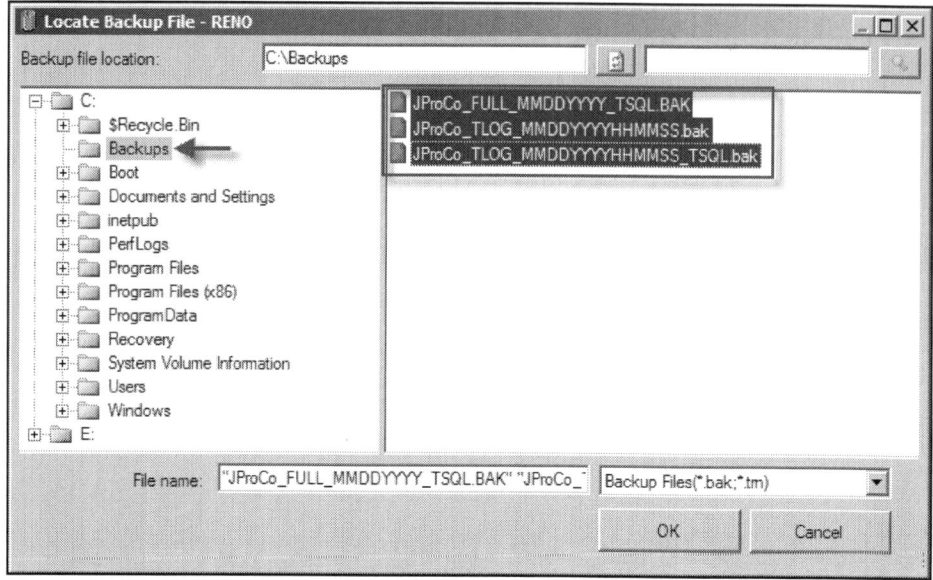

Figure 5.10 Browse to C:\Backups, select the files and click **OK**.

This returns us back to the **Restore Database** window. Click on the **Files** page to see that we can change the location of where to restore the data and log files. In some situations we may have to restore a database to a server that does not have the exact same disk configuration. We also may want to restore the files to a location other than the default location for that instance. (Figure 5.11)

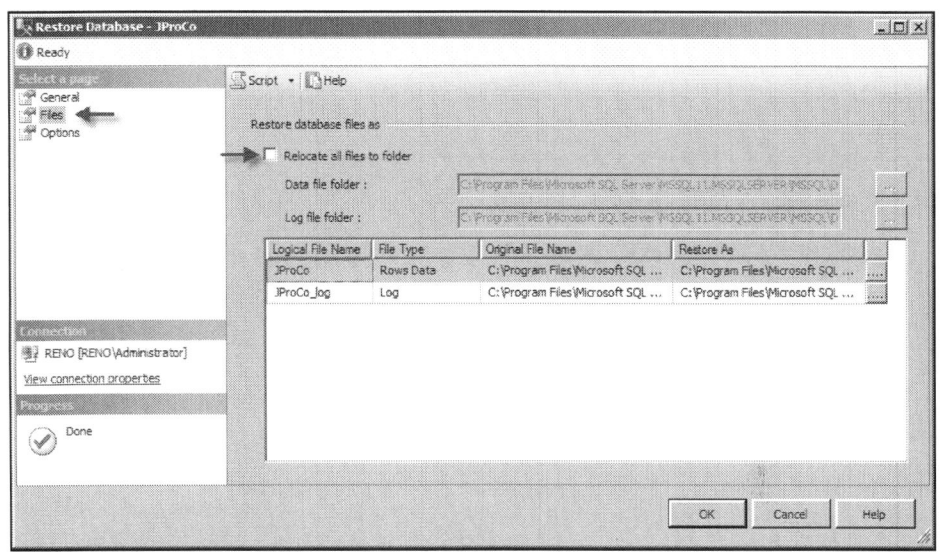

Figure 5.11 The **Files** page is where we can change the location to restore the database files.

Now click on the **Options** page. (Figure 5.12) On this page we have a number of restore options to choose from. Check the box to **Overwrite the existing database (WITH REPLACE)**.

This is where we could leave the database offline so that additional restores can be applied or bring the database online. Next to **Recovery state**, choose the option that states **RESTORE WITH RECOVERY**) since we will not be restoring any additional files. Next uncheck the box to **Take tail-log backup before restore**. This particular option in the restore dialog is new to SQL Server 2012. We will be covering tail-log backup terminology in Chapter 5.

Nobody should be connected to or using this database until we are done with the restore. There might be some system connections that should be told to disconnect during this restore. We can close any existing connections to the database by checking the box **Close existing connections to destination database**.

Chapter 5 Transaction Log Backups

READER NOTE: *I typically like to check for existing connections using the SP_WHO2 system stored procedure to ensure I am not affecting any active users.*

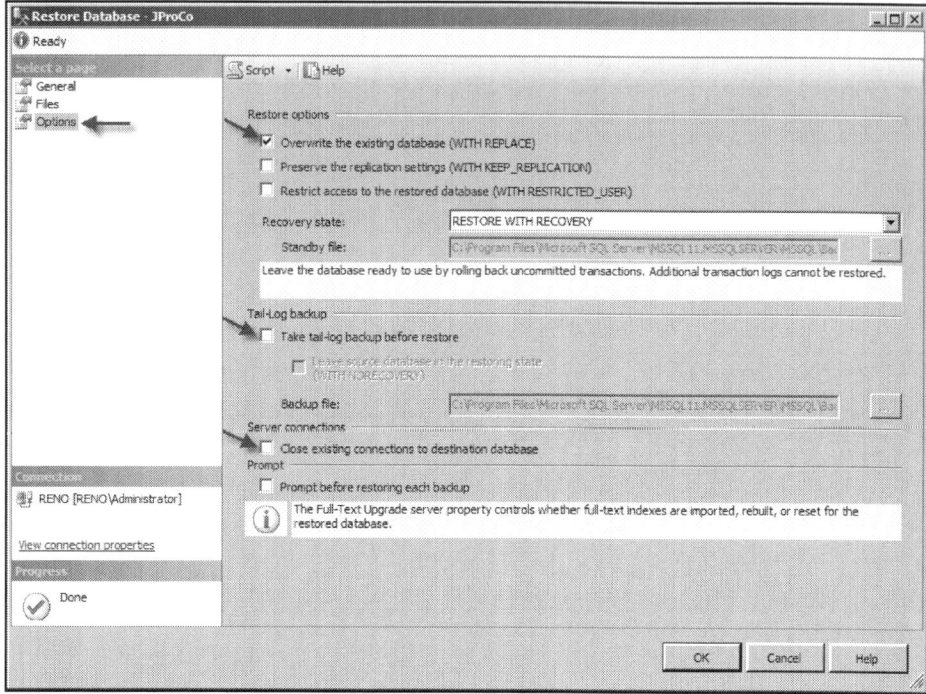

Figure 5.12 Restore Database Options Page.

We are now ready to restore the JProCo database full and transaction log backups. Click **OK**. (Figure 5.13)

Figure 5.13 The JProCo database has been restored.

Restoring Using T-SQL

The preferred choice for performing restores is to use T-SQL. Although DBAs keep scripts handy for performing full and differential restores, it is a little more tedious to restore transaction logs. It is a good idea to still keep a script handy however depending on how many transaction logs there are to restore. It can be a daunting task to script all of them out the first time. It is still much easier using T-SQL than restoring them one by one using the graphical UI.

Just like with restoring a differential backup, we have to restore the full backup that the transaction logs belong to before we can begin restoring the transaction log or logs.

The syntax for a transaction log restore using T-SQL is like this:

RESTORE LOG DB_NAME FROM <backup_device> WITH <options>

There are several options that we can use after the WITH statement. We can specify the recovery setting RECOVERY / NORECOVERY. In our case we need to restore our first transaction log with NORECOVERY, and then we will restore our last transaction log with RECOVERY. Since the default when we restore is WITH RECOVERY, we will need to take a moment to specify NORECOVERY. For this example, let's execute the T-SQL code below substituting the ***JProCo_TLOG*** backup name:

```
USE [MASTER]
GO
RESTORE DATABASE JProCo
FROM DISK =
  'C:\Backups\JProCo_Full_MMDDYYYY.BAK'
WITH NORECOVERY

RESTORE LOG JProCo
FROM DISK =
  'C:\Backups\JProCo_TLOG_MMDDYYYYHHMMSS.BAK'
WITH RECOVERY
```

Notice that we only restored the first transaction log that we made. This first transaction log was before we inserted the record adding Muhammad

Wong as a contractor. Let's run our query again to show that Mr. Wong does not exist in our database:

```
SELECT LastName, FirstName
FROM JProCo.[dbo].[Contractor]
WHERE LastName = 'Wong' AND FirstName = 'Muhammad'
```

This should get a received "(0 row(s) affected)". Since we have restored our JProCo database **WITH RECOVERY** we cannot restore the last transaction log. This is a very common issue when performing real life restores. A risk when performing multiple restores to bring a database online is accidentally restoring **WITH RECOVERY** when we don't mean to. Unfortunately we cannot set the database back into a recovery state. We must start the restore back over beginning with the full backup. We will have to restore the full backup **WITH NORECOVERY**, the second transaction log **WITH NORECOVERY** and then our final transaction log **WITH RECOVERY**. Let's give that a try now:

```
USE [MASTER]
GO
RESTORE DATABASE JProCo
FROM DISK = 'C:\Backups\JProCo_Full_MMDDYYYY.BAK'
WITH NORECOVERY

RESTORE LOG JProCo
FROM DISK =
  'C:\Backups\JProCo_TLOG_MMDDYYYYHHMMSS.BAK'
WITH NORECOVERY

RESTORE LOG JProCo
FROM DISK =
  'C:\Backups\JProCo_TLOG_MMDDYYYYHHMMSS_TSQL.BAK'
WITH RECOVERY
```

In this example we restored both transaction logs. We added a new record after the first log backup but before the second log backup was taken. Since we just restored our full backup that does not contain our new contractor and then restored the second transaction log that contained it, let's confirm it is in fact in our database. Execute the following script:

```sql
SELECT LastName, FirstName
FROM JProCo.[dbo].[Contractor]
WHERE LastName = 'Wong' AND FirstName = 'Muhammad'
```

We should now have "(1 row(s) affected)" and can see Muhammad Wong listed in the database.

Summary

Adding transaction log backups into the backup routine for transactional databases is probably the single most important thing we can do as a database professional. If the organization has an expectation to perform a point in time restore of an environment then we need to get this done. If we cannot because we don't have adequate backups this falls short of the SLA. Two of the primary benefits of having adequate transaction log backups are keeping the size of the transaction log small and still having a point in time recovery. Without making regular transaction log backups on a database in the full recovery model, the transaction log will continue to grow until it runs out of drive space.

In order to be able to restore the transaction logs, we must first restore the last known good full backup and then the transaction logs in the order they were taken. Performing the restores utilizing the graphical UI can be time consuming, as we must restore them one at a time. Utilizing T-SQL for the restores can be much quicker for the Admin to implement if they are ready ahead of time.

Points to Ponder
Transaction Log Backup

1. Transaction log backups can only be made on databases using the bulk-logged or full recovery model.
2. Before the first transaction log backup can be made, at least one full backup must have been completed.

3. Each transaction log backup contains the transaction log records since the previous transaction log backup.
4. Transaction log backups issue a checkpoint, which is a way of marking a transaction as completed and officially saved to the database.
5. Data in the transaction log that has had a checkpoint is stored in two places (the transaction log and the database).
6. Transaction log backups issue a checkpoint, which allow the transaction log to free up space to be reused by moving that data to the next transaction log backup.
7. If we are restoring a database on the same server that took the backup then the msdb will remember the order and types of our backups and make a relevant restore suggestion.
8. Because of msdb, when we use the graphical UI and we choose restore database, the most recent backup history will be displayed. On that screen we can choose which backups to restore.

Review Quiz – Chapter Five

1.) What restore sequence is correct for restoring transaction logs?

   O a. Full, differential, transaction logs.
   O b. Differential, full, transaction logs.
   O c. Full, transaction logs, differential.
   O d. Full, incremental, transaction logs.

2.) Restoring multiple transaction logs on a failover server is more efficient using the graphical UI because it can chain multiple transaction logs and restore them at once. TRUE/FALSE?

   O a. TRUE
   O b. FALSE

3.) Transaction logs must be restored in the sequence they were taken. TRUE/FALSE

   O a. TRUE
   O b. FALSE

Answer Key

1.) The restore sequence is full, differential (if we make them), then the transaction logs in the order they were taken, therefore (a) is the correct answer.

2.) On a failover server msdb would not contain the backup history for the database we are restoring so we would have to specify one file at a time to restore them. It would be much quicker to specify the files in order in a T-SQL script to restore them; therefore (b) is the correct answer.

3.) Transaction logs must be restored based on the LSN sequence, so they must be restored in order; therefore (a) is the correct answer.

Chapter 6.   Common Restore Strategies

As database administrators we have to know what is expected of us. More specifically we must know our SLAs. We have a great responsibility to manage and maintain the data assets of our organizations.

With the high number of options for types of backups, we also have a multitude of options for a restore strategy. In fact there are more types of backups in SQL Server than we have covered so far. With options such as full, differential, transaction log, file, and file group backups we can end up with quite a few different restore strategies.

The restore strategy will depend on the backup strategy. If we are only making a full backup weekly on Sunday night for a system with data that changes daily, we can only recover up to the most recent Sunday. We will not be able to restore to a point in time mid-week.

There are a few things we must have in order to create a proper backup and recovery solution. First we must know what is expected of us (what is our SLA). A bigger database might take more time to restore from a full backup than a smaller database. While the database is down the people around us can get really edgy until it's backed up. How long does it take to restore a database? In technical terms we need to ask what is the Recovery Time Objective (RTO).

If we can get the database back in 30 minutes, that might be considered very good for some companies. Grabbing the last full backup from Sunday will take less time than grabbing the Sunday full and yesterday's differential but taking that extra time puts back three more days of valuable data. Getting three more days of data means you get a more recent point of time recovery. Waiting 10 more minutes to save three days makes sense. Therefore RTO is not the only SLA. How current we can restore the database is the Recovery Point Object (RPO).

Out of RTO and RPO, this book is most concerned with RPO for the backup and recovery solution. The recovery point can be more easily translated to "How much data can the company afford to lose". The recovery time objective is most often a financial decision. If there is an RPO of 15 minutes, transaction log backups every 15 minutes with

Chapter 6 Common Restore Strategies

shipping the logs offsite will make this SLA. On the other hand if we have an RTO of 15 minutes, then there will be additional hardware cost like a live failover system or cluster. Low RTOs usually involves building out the environment in a second datacenter to mirror the first SQL server.

SQL Server has different ways it can treat the recent data stored in its log files. Most often it will save the checkpoint data until we back up the log. The log file grows until the backup is done and then the backup starts it over as an empty log file. It's kind of like taking out the trash each week.

The default recovery model of SQL Server is to hold on to the data. If this data were not saved in the transaction log then there would be no log to backup. The only choices would be full or differential. If recovery is not an issue and the goal is to keep the log file small we can choose the transaction log to truncate all data on the checkpoint. This is a fancy way of saying the transaction log will not hold on to any data that it is not currently working on. No storage of data. Truncating the log on checkpoint happens when we set the recovery model to simple mode.

Based on the backup needs, the databases will have to have the correct recovery model. If the database is in simple mode, then we will not be able to make any transaction log backups. We would still be able to schedule full and differential backups while using the simple recovery mode. For some companies with a relaxed RPO this may be an adequate solution. There is no one solution that fits all situations for backup and recovery. Most often the safest solution is one that also includes regular transaction log backups, however in some situations this could be over kill and use up valuable resources when not needed. The best thing we can do is have the business define their needs and architect a solution to meet and exceed their requirement.

Let's now explore some possible scenarios and strategies. The following sections will list out the various scenarios and define the RPO they provide.

READER NOTE: *For the exercises in this chapter a folder needs to be created called Backups on the local C: drive (C:\Backups). Please run the script SQLBackupSetup01.sql in order to follow along with the examples* for this chapter. All scripts mentioned in this chapter may be found in the "Solution Series" section at www.Joes2Pros.com.

Full Backup Only

If a full backup is the only type of backup in the overall backup solution, that would indicate we can either recreate any daily work lost or that no data is changing on a daily basis. This is an adequate solution for those two scenarios. If the database does have some form of data changing throughout the day that cannot be easily recreated then we need a more robust backup solution.

Full Backup with Differential Backups

Full backups with differential backups can do a couple of things for us. First if we are performing weekly full with daily differentials we are decreasing the amount of data that has to be re-entered on a daily basis. For a Recovery Point Objective (RPO) this does not give us any increased benefit as compared to taking daily full backups but saving storage space.

If we are making multiple per day differential backups then this decreases the RPO by the amount of the time difference of the differential backups. An example of where this would be beneficial would be if we have a system that only imports data every 4 hours to be backed up every 4 hours. If we perform nightly full backups and scheduled a differential every 4 hours (one for each 4 hour data load) then we are protected.

Full with Transaction Log Backups

The most common backup and recovery solution for OLTP databases is nightly full backups with transaction log backups at a short interval. Common time frames are 1 hour, 30 minutes, 15 minutes, 10 minutes and 5 minutes.

The more frequent the transaction log backups occur, the more transaction logs we will be dealing with during a restore. If we have been following along in the book and participated in the exercises in Chapter 5 we will know that this could be a very time consuming task. This takes time using either the graphical UI or T-SQL (if we had to write out each and every transaction log to restore).

There is a much simpler way to create the restore script. Msdb stores all backup history for every database. The two tables to take a look at are `MSDB.dbo.backupset` and `MSDB.dbo.backupmediafamily`. We can join these two tables together and generate a robust script that will get the last full backup and each transaction log backup since the most recent full. In the backupset table, the "type" field lists the type of backup. Full = 'D', Differential = 'I' and transaction = 'L'. We can show a small result set to demonstrate what this data looks like. Run the following script:

```
SELECT TOP 10
  b.type,
  b.database_name,
  mf.physical_device_name
FROM msdb.dbo.backupset b
  JOIN msdb.dbo.backupmediafamily mf
ON b.media_set_id = mf.media_set_id
ORDER BY backup_set_id DESC
```

We will get a similar result set to Figure 6.1. The result set below shows us that the backup set "type" for full is "D", differential is "I", and transaction log is "L".

	type	database_name	physical_device_name
1	L	JProCo	C:\Backups\JProCo_TLOG_MMDDYYYYHHMMSS_TSQL.bak
2	I	JProCo	C:\Backups\JProCo_DIFF_MMDDYYYY_TSQL.BAK
3	D	JProCo	C:\Backups\JProCo_FULL_MMDDYYYY_TSQL.BAK

Figure 6.1 Sampling of data.

With some basic T-SQL skills we can have it generate the restore scripts. We have included a sample script in the resources folder called

(RESTORE_SCRIPT_FULL_W_TLOG.SQL). When we execute this script for the database we wish to restore, it will query msdb and get the most recent full backup and each transaction log backup since that full backup was taken. Each restore uses the WITH NORECOVERY with a final script that restores the database WITH RECOVERY to bring it online. A sample of the result set can be seen in Figure 6.2. All we would do is copy the script column and paste it into our query window and then execute the scripts. Imagine this was a production system that was making transaction log backups every 5 minutes. In 10 hours that would be 120 transaction log backups. That would take a while to write the restore script.

	backup_set_id	Script
1	1185	RESTORE DATABASE JProCo FROM DISK = 'C:\Backups\JProCo_FULL_MMDDYYYY_TSQL.BAK' WITH NORECOVERY
2	1187	RESTORE LOG JProCo FROM DISK = 'C:\Backups\JProCo_TLOG_MMDDYYYYHHMMSS_TSQL.bak' WITH NORECOVERY
3	999999999	RESTORE DATABASE JProCo WITH RECOVERY

Figure 6.2 Result set sample for full backup with transaction log.

It is recommended that we add a step to each of the backup jobs to create the restore script as we make the backups. Even if the directory structure is different on the server we are performing the restore on, we can easily do a **find and replace** to update drive letters and paths. Having a script per database that writes to a directory that is backed up with our database backups can drastically decrease the complexity and the time it takes to begin the actual restore process.

Full, Differential, Transaction Log

Using a nightly full, daily differential and regularly scheduled transaction log backups are also a very common solution. It provides the same level of protection as nightly full and transaction log backups, however it helps to reduce the time the daily backups take by only backing up the changed data. As we covered in Chapter 4, having differential backups in the backup routine means we have to restore the full backup, then restore the latest differential, and then any transaction logs since that differential. It is also possible to restore the full backup, then all the transaction logs since the full. This would be much more time consuming than just restoring the full, most recent differential, and then the remaining logs.

The exact thing applies here as it does with nightly full and transaction log backups. Restoring the full backup and then the differential is the easy task, applying the transaction log backups are the time consuming task (since there are often many and they need to be done in order). The same process for utilizing msdb to gather the last full, differential and then all transaction logs since the most recent differential apply here as well. We have included a sample script in the resources folder called (**RESTORE_SCRIPT_FULL_DIFF_W_TLOG.SQL**). When we execute this script for the database we wish to restore, it will query msdb for that database. When it does, it gets the most recent full backup, the most recent differential since the last full, and each transaction log backup since the last differential was taken. Each restore uses the WITH NORECOVERY until the final script. The final restore uses the WITH RECOVERY. An example of the result set can be seen in Figure 6.3.

	backup_set_id	Script
1	1185	RESTORE DATABASE JProCo FROM DISK = 'C:\Backups\JProCo_FULL_MMDDYYYY_TSQL.BAK' WITH NORECOVERY
2	1186	RESTORE DATABASE JProCo FROM DISK = 'C:\Backups\JProCo_DIFF_MMDDYYYY_TSQL.BAK' WITH NORECOVERY
3	1187	RESTORE LOG JProCo FROM DISK = 'C:\Backups\JProCo_TLOG_MMDDYYYYHHMMSS_TSQL.bak' WITH NORECOVERY
4	999999999	RESTORE DATABASE JProCo WITH RECOVERY

Figure 6.3 Result set sample for full, differential, and transaction logs.

Having a step in the backup job to script out the restore script to a file is key to being able to quickly have the restore scripts ready.

Summary

As a database administrator our primary responsibility is likely to be to protect the data. That means that we need to be able to recover the database in the event of a disaster or data quality issue.

If we take only full backups then our restore strategy is to use the most recent full backup. If we are taking full and differential backups then we just need the most recent full and the most recent differential. If we are taking full, differential, and log backups then we need to use the most recent full and the most recent differential followed by every transaction log backup in order after the last differential.

The SLA (Service Level Agreement) of the system will determine the type of backup and recovery solution needed. In other words, do what the company needs. With determining the backup solution, the key objective is to be able to meet or exceed the Recovery Point Objective (RPO). The question to ask the business units is "How much data can we afford to lose?". The first answer we will get is usually "none/zero" data loss. We will have to kindly present the challenges and hardware costs that zero data loss comes with.

Live clustering failover systems with near zero data loss often triple the hardware costs for your company. Try to explain how reasonable and low cost it is to allow for 15 minutes or less of data loss. In many cases that is acceptable. There have been a few circumstances where that was not tolerable and we made adjustments such as decreasing the time between transaction log backups from 15 minutes to 5.

Organizations are spending much more time and money to ensure that their critical systems are highly available. With SQL Server there are several technologies that can be applied to mitigate the risk of extended downtime. High availability (like clusters and failover servers) however is not disaster recovery. Recovery Time Objective (RTO) dictates how quickly the database would need to be recovered or roughly translated as "How long can the system be down?". Usually systems that have an established RTO have a dedicated system set up for disaster recovery.

Many people think asynchronous database mirroring is a disaster recovery solution. Database mirroring involves having a dedicated server in place that provides a hot standby on a database-by-database basis. Database mirroring unfortunately is not suitable for disaster recovery. Think about a scenario where a table was accidently dropped. In a mirror setup, the table is also dropped on the secondary server. To recover from that situation a restore from a backup is the only option.

Our RTO is a measurement of how long it takes to notice an issue, report the issue, notify the person to correct the issue, and the response time of the person to correct the issue. The response time of the person making the correction may involve travel time to the office or their home, the time to remote in, time to access the situation, and the time it takes to perform the necessary actions to recover. If the restore process takes 1 hour, how many extra minutes are involved in the notification process, travel time, etc.? This additional time should be factored in to the recovery solutions.

Whatever backup and recovery plan we put in place, we need to test it and test it often. We don't want to be in a situation where we are recovering a critical system and the CXO asks how long it is going to take to restore if we don't even know ourselves. Wouldn't it be much nicer to pull out a log and tell the CXO that the last time this was performed (within a month or so) that it took X number of minutes?

Points to Ponder
Common Restore Strategies

1. When we have multiple files to restore, each restore uses the WITH NORECOVERY until the final statement. The final restore uses the WITH RECOVERY.

2. If we had 10 backup files to restore (1 full, 1 differential, and 8 transaction log backups) then the full, differential and the first 7 transaction log backups would be NORECOVERY and the last transaction log backup would be RECOVERY.

3. Backups are only valid if they can be restored. Without a regular process to validate our backups we are more likely to suffer extended downtime and potential data loss.

4. It is entirely possible to recover a database from an initial full backup and every transaction log since the full was taken. In scenarios with a weekly full backup, daily differential and transaction log backups every 10 minutes; we could restore the full backup and each transaction log backup skipping the differentials. It would take much more time and be more complex, but if we did not have the differentials it is possible.

5. Whichever backup strategy we use, it should be fully tested to ensure it meets the Service Level Agreement of the organization. Being able to technically restore a database in a way that that falls well outside of the SLA could mean the difference in the company staying open for business or closing its doors.

6. In the backupset table, the "type" field lists the type of backup. Full = 'D', Differential = 'I' and Transaction = 'L'.

7. If a database is 500 GB in size and the RTO is 60 minutes. Chances are we can't be notified, connect to the remote server and restore from backup within 60 minutes. If log shipping had been configured with a 24-hour load delay we could easily roll the logs forward up to seconds before the issue that is causing us to have to restore. The transaction logs from the 24-hour period of time would be far less than the 500 GB full backup plus the logs since the backup was taken.

Review Quiz – Chapter SIX

1.) RPO stands for _____?

    O a. Recovery Process Owner
    O b. Recovery Product Object
    O c. Recovered Process Online
    O d. Recovery Point Objective

2.) A restore script can be created by using the data stored in msdb.

    O a. TRUE
    O b. FALSE

3.) For a high transaction database, which option gives the most protection for recovering data with the least amount of data loss?

    O a. Weekly full backups, daily differential with transaction log backups every 15 minutes.
    O b. Nightly full backups.
    O c. Weekly full backups, daily differential.

O d. Nightly full, differential every 4 hours.

Answer Key

1.) RPO = Recovery Point Objective, so (d) is the answer.

2.) Msdb records every backup operation, so the answer is (a) TRUE.

3.) Weekly full backups with daily differential and transaction log backups every 15 minutes will only allow for up to 15 minutes of data loss, so (a) is the correct answer.

Chapter 7.   Copy Backup

Anyone who was a teen in the 80s is fully aware of what it is like to make a copy. We used to make copies of cassette tapes of our favorite music. Making mixed tapes was a really big thing to do. When compact discs came out it was a little harder to make our mixed cd but we soon figured it out. Photo copy machines became main-stream as well. Now when people have to go to a library to do research they can make a photocopy of the few pages they need and go back to their own place to do their term paper. Being able to make a copy of those pages in the book, or making a copy of their favorite music did not alter the original item. SQL Server has the ability to make a backup without affecting the original data as well.

In SQL Server 2005 and above there is an option to make a backup using WITH COPY_ONLY. As we learned in previous chapters, when SQL Server makes a backup it is tracking these backups using an LSN. So what is a copy backup? This COPY_ONLY backup will back up all the data in our database without resetting any of the differential bitmaps (AKA the backup markers). It also does not alter the size or flow of the existing transaction log. Because of this the copy backup has no effect on the sequence of backups of the next differential or log file taking place during the week. I like to tell people that it is a backup that never happened.

Why is a COPY_ONLY backup important? If our organization is utilizing differential backups, those backups are dependent on the previous full backup. Let's assume our organization is using weekly full, daily differential and hourly transaction log backups. Now imagine that a member of our team is asked to make a current full backup of a production database to be used in Dev or QA on a Tuesday morning. Your team member (being the nice person they are) makes a full backup on Tuesday night and restores it to the QA server. Later in the week on Thursday there is a problem with the production database and the team has to restore from backup. You are the person that has to perform the restore so you grab the Sunday night's full and Wednesday night's differential right? When you try to apply Wednesday's differential you get a nasty error telling you that the differential does not apply to that full backup you just restored. There is a Tuesday full backup that was taken that nobody else knows about.

Chapter 7 Copy Backup

After asking the team, everyone finds out that another backup had been taken since Sunday, but the person who made the backup has deleted it. What are the options now?

We might not be totally out of luck but it will take a lot more work to get up and running. If we are fortunate enough to have kept enough of the transaction logs we can apply all the transaction logs since the last full backup. That is about 100 restores that need to be done (one incremental per hour since Sunday). The scripts that we learned in Chapter 6 would be most helpful in this situation. Creating a script manually of four days' worth of transaction logs can be a time consuming task.

What should have been done on Tuesday night? The way we can prevent these types of situations when we need a complete backup of the database at an ad-hoc time is to always use WITH COPY_ONLY. Whenever we make any backups outside of our regularly scheduled backups. COPY_ONLY also applies to transaction log backups. COPY_ONLY backups for transaction logs do not truncate the log, which is very important.

If using COPY_ONLY with DIFFERENTIAL, the COPY_ONLY is ignored and a differential backup is taken.

READER NOTE: *For the exercises in this chapter a folder needs to be created called Backups on the local C: drive (C:\Backups). Please run the script SQLBackupSetup01.sql in order to follow along with the examples for this chapter. All scripts mentioned in this chapter may be found in the "Solution Series" section at www.Joes2Pros.com.*

Using the Graphical UI

Using the graphical UI to make a copy backup is much the same as using the graphical UI to make a full backup. The restores are exactly the same as well. To make a COPY_ONLY backup using the graphical UI within SSMS we need to follow the steps outlined in Chapter 3 with one change. First, right-click on the database we want to backup and choose **Tasks** > and then the **Back Up...** option. Do this now with JProCo. (Figure 7.1)

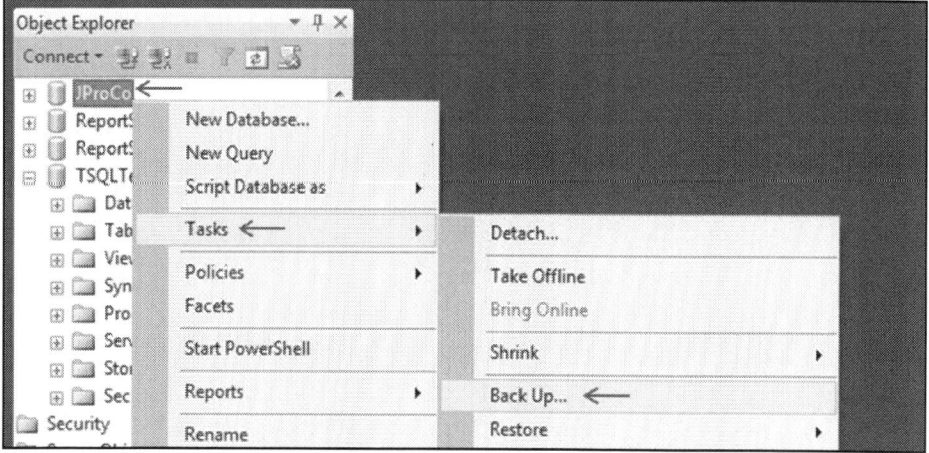

Figure 7.1 Right click on the database, choose **Tasks** and then **Back Up...**

The **General** page of the window appears where we can make a number of selections. If we were to select **OK** at this point, it will make a full backup of the database into the default backup location for the SQL Server instance. In Figure 7.2 the first option is to choose the database to be backed up. Next is the backup type we wish to make, in this case we want to select **Full**. Check the option for **Copy-only Backup**. For **Backup component** we want to ensure **Database** is selected and under **Backup set** we can specify the **Name** of the backup set, typically we would just accept the default value here. The next item is the destination and name of the backup file. The default path is set at the instance level. For SQL 2012 the default location is:

C:\Program Files\Microsoft SQL Server\MSSQL11.MSSQLSERVER\MSSQL\Backup\.

Chapter 7 Copy Backup

For this example we want to replace that value so click **Remove** > **Add**.

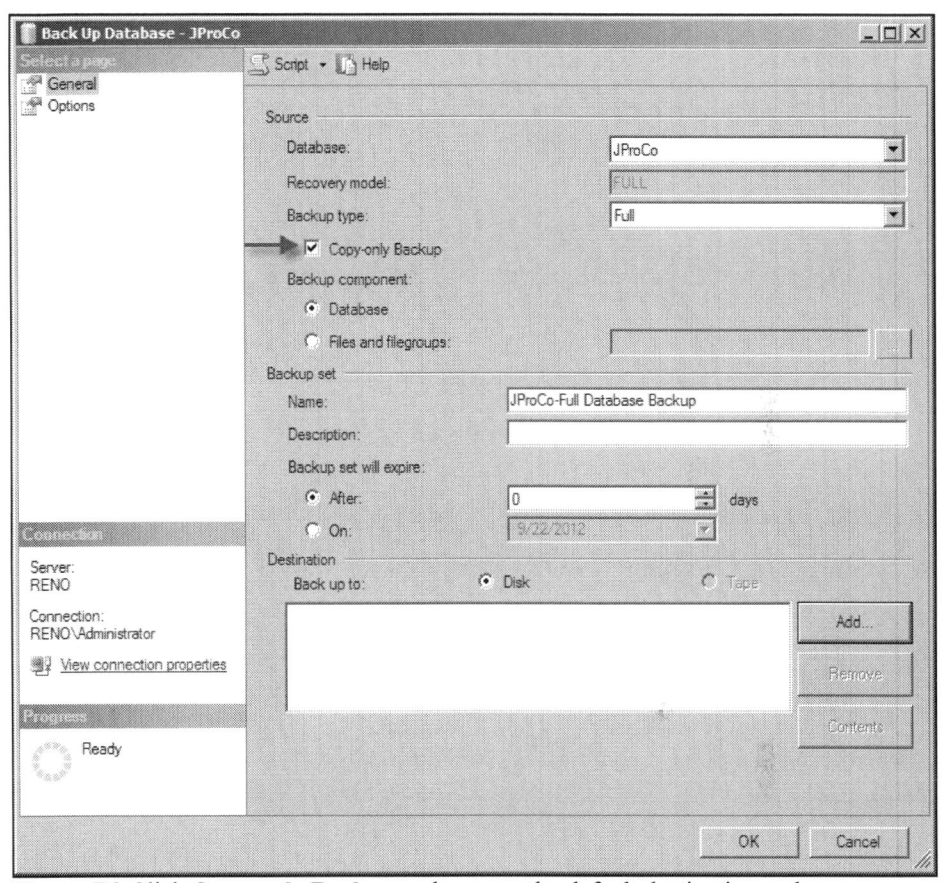

Figure 7.2 Click **Copy-only Backup** and remove the default destination path so you can add your own path.

Type the path and name of the database backup file. (Figure 7.3) As with all the backups we make, it is good practice to have the date and time included in the backup name in addition to the backup type. Type the path and name of the database file. Replace MMDDYYYY with actual date value in the form of Month Day Year. For example if today is May 16th 2013 then the filename should be
JProCo_COPY_ONLY_05162013.BAK. This gives a nice visual aid rather than having to look at the timestamp on the file itself. Now click **OK**.

Chapter 7 Copy Backup

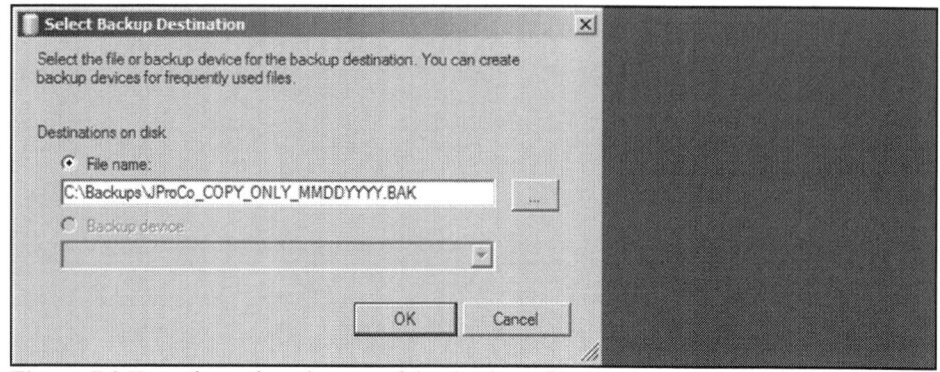

Figure 7.3 Type the path and name of the database file. Replace MMDDYYYY with actual date value in the form of Month Day Year.

Click the **Options** page to see that we have several more options to choose. Figure 7.4 shows the default values. **Overwrite media** defaults to **Append to the existing backup set**. Just like with full backups, COPY_ONLY backups must be verified by restoring them regularly. It is still recommend to **Verify backup when finished** however that does not mean the backup file is 100% valid. In most cases we are making a COPY_ONLY backup in order to immediately restore it to another server. COPY_ONLY backups are typically not part of a scheduled backup and recovery plan. Compression is also an option with COPY_ONLY backups and performs the same way as it does with other backups. We will use the default option here as we did in the previous chapters. Click **OK** and the JProCo database will backup to:
C:\Backups\JProCo_COPY_ONLY_MMDDYYYY.BAK.

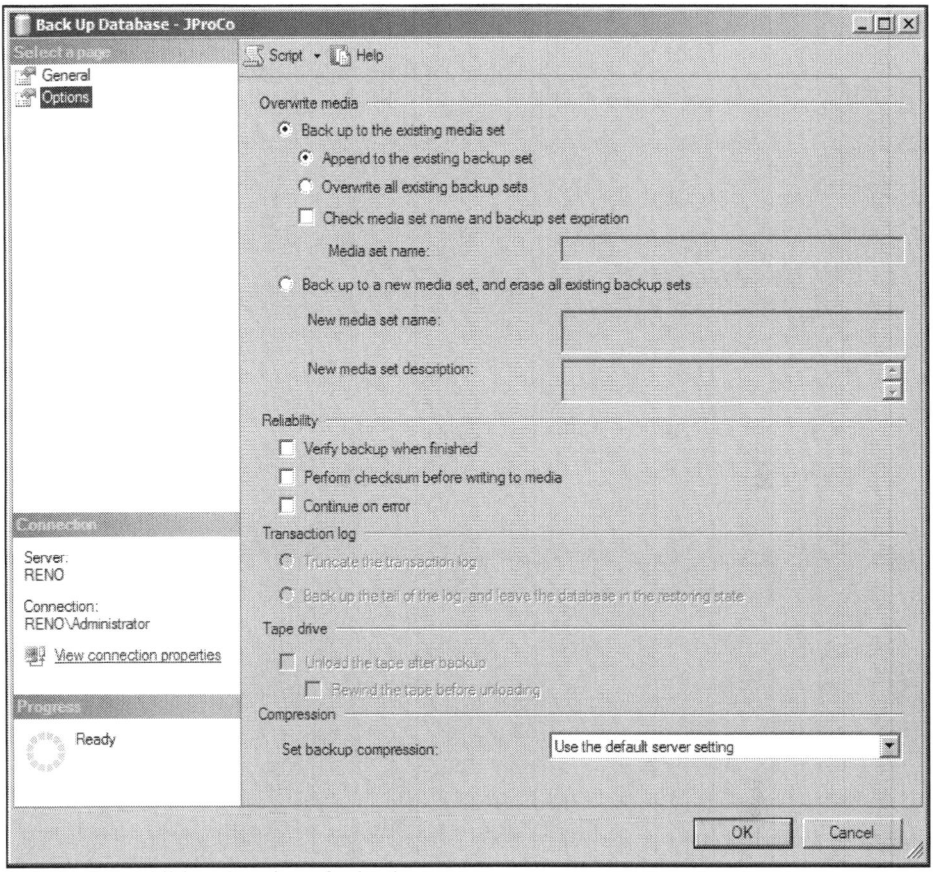

Chapter 7 Copy Backup

Figure 7.4 Additional options for backups.

Using T-SQL

We covered the benefits of using T-SQL in Chapter 3 explaining how having to check so many boxes each time we do a backup can be cumbersome. Creating a COPY_ONLY backup is no different. The syntax is exactly the same as used in Chapter 3 with the exception of adding the COPY_ONLY option and naming our backup file according to the backup type. Being able to save this script for reuse at a later time makes it the preferred choice for making COPY_ONLY backups.

The syntax is very straightforward. We specify:

BACKUP DATABASE DB_NAME TO <backup_device> WITH <options>

and then specify the options needed. Since we are making a COPY_ONLY backup we have to specify WITH COPY_ONLY. Let's include _TSQL at the end of the file name to not use the same name we did in the graphical UI.

Let's go ahead and make a full backup by using the following script:

```
BACKUP DATABASE JProCo TO DISK =
  'C:\Backups\JProCo_COPY_ONLY_MMDDYYYY_TSQL.BAK'
WITH COPY_ONLY
```

Restoring a Copy Backup

The copy backup file itself is not any different than a regular full, differential or transaction log backup. Since the backup otherwise does not behave any different, the restore process is exactly the same.

Summary

Using COPY_ONLY backups help maintain the backup and restore chain. They should be mandatory for one-off backups in organizations that utilize differential backups. To make COPY_ONLY backups the process is exactly the same as making full backups, but simply choosing the COPY_ONLY option.

Points to Ponder Copy Backup

1. If we want to take an ad-hoc full backup of our database and not have it reset the differential bitmaps we can use the WITH COPY_ONLY option on the backup.

2. Copy Only backups should be a standard option being used if we make backups outside of our regular backup cycle.

3. Backups do not cause blocking contrary to any myths out there, however backups are very I/O intensive which can cause performance issues related to I/O if they are run during high peak times.
4. COPY_ONLY backups can be made on all recovery models.
5. A COPY_ONLY backup cannot be used as a differential backup.
6. Using the COPY_ONLY option on backups of transaction logs does not truncate the log. Using COPY_ONLY on a differential backup, the COPY_ONLY option is ignored and a differential backup is taken.
7. Restoring a backup that was made with the COPY_ONLY option is not any different than restoring the same type of backup without the COPY_ONLY option.

Review Quiz – Chapter Seven

1.) A COPY_ONLY backup of a transaction log truncates the log.

O a. TRUE
O b. FALSE

2.) The COPY_ONLY option can be used to make a COPY_ONLY differential backup.

O a. TRUE
O b. FALSE

3.) COPY_ONLY backups do not impact the sequence of backups.

O a. TRUE
O b. FALSE

Answer Key

1.) Transaction log backups with the option COPY_ONLY do not truncate the log therefore (b) is the correct answer.

Chapter 7 Copy Backup

2.) Using COPY_ONLY with a differential backup causes the COPY_ONLY option to be ignored and a differential backup is taken, therefore (b) is the correct answer.

3.) COPY_ONLY backups do not impact the sequence of backups, that is their unique feature, therefore (a) is the correct answer.

Chapter 8. File and Filegroup

Organization is a part of our day-to-day lives. Without structure and organization our lives would be chaos. Even in the simplest forms organization helps us to be more efficient. Let's think about where we store our clothes for a moment. Most of us have a drawer for our under garments, a separate drawer for socks, maybe one for under shirts, one for shorts and so forth. These drawers may be messy, but certain items are always stored in their specific place. How chaotic would our mornings be if we had to search multiple drawers for a pair of socks only to find one color sock in one drawer and the matching sock in another?

In SQL Server there often comes a time when we have to split our very large databases (VLDB), into multiple file groups. How large does a database have to be in order to be considered a VLDB is debatable but a general consensus is that anything nearing or exceeding 1TB in size is safe to call a VLDB. A key issue with VLDBs is the time it takes to back them up each night. Many times the backup does not fit within the standard backup window and the backup runs into production hours thus impacting production performance due to the I/O strain it can put on the disk and network. If daily backups take more than 24 hours to run then this is a sign that another solution is needed.

At some point in our career as a database administrator we will most likely find ourselves having to manage a VLDB. Either we will have to tame one by possibly splitting it into multiple file groups using the existing database design, or we may find ourselves having to partition very large tables.

Before jumping straight into trying to split the database into file groups, we should first check the data being stored to make sure we are only keeping the data within the retention period. How old is the oldest data in the database? Often times there are companies with systems that do not purge their data regularly. For these systems a purge may be all that is needed to get them back to a manageable size. When this is not the case, we should forecast how large the database is expected to grow and then work with the DBAs to come up with a long-term plan. Often this involves partitioning the database. By partitioning the data into multiple filegroups we can better manage the data from index optimizations, backups, restores, and performance improvements. In the cases I have encountered either the design of the database already accounted for storing the data in quarterly tables or there were only a couple of tables that utilized the majority of the space in the database.

In the case of the database with quarterly tables I was able to easily move the tables into yearly filegroups, with the databases with very large tables with date/time columns I used a partition function to split the data into yearly file groups. It should be noted here that these activities should always be thoroughly tested and approved by the vendors whose databases we are working with.

Another nice benefit of multiple filegroups is that we can place the filegroups on separate disk arrays thus improving the overall disk I/O. This also gives us the ability to place really old archive data on a slower disk thus saving the organization money by moving less read data onto a cheaper and slower disk. High performance enterprise storage cost range from $5,000 - $10,000 (USD) per usable terabyte. Slower performing tier 3 storage ranges from $1,000 - $3,000 (USD) per usable terabyte.

File and filegroup backups operate no differently and for the most part are the same concept. Making a filegroup backup will backup up each file in that file group just as specifying each file individually. When creating a file or filegroup backup we can back up the entire file or filegroup or perform differential backups.

After a major disaster (such as a hurricane, earthquake, tornado or tsunami) utility companies have a great deal of work to do. In most of the cases above there are massive power outages across a very large region. The utility companies have to mobilize and begin work on restoring power. What is the best way for them to accomplish this task? Should they disperse and work in very small groups trying to clear trees and put up new poles and power lines, or should different groups team up and work together to restore power to the more critical areas first? Putting their effort at restoring the critical areas first is the best way to start restoring power to their customers.

Chapter 8 File and Filegroup

An example of being able to quickly restore service to a VLDB that has multiple file groups is being able to perform piecemeal restores. Online piecemeal restores became available with SQL 2005 Enterprise Edition (Developer Edition too). A piecemeal restore allows us the ability to make the database partially available by restoring the PRIMARY file group first. Secondary filegroups can then be restored at a later time. With Enterprise Edition we can restore the secondary file groups without taking the PRIMARY offline. With Standard Edition we can still perform a piecemeal restore, however restoring the secondary filegroups is an offline operation.

When performing file-based restores, we must have the accompanying transaction log backups in order to be able to roll forward each file backup. The only times where transaction logs are not needed are in the case of files in a read-only filegroup. Due to the need to have transaction logs, the database will need to be in the full recovery model.

There are several methods and justifications for using files or filegroups with SQL Server. The intent of this chapter is not to give a lesson in partitioning the database. What this chapter is intended to do is present the methods to backup and restore using file and filegroup backups.

READER NOTE: *For the exercises in this chapter a folder needs to be created called Backups on the local C: drive (C:\Backups). Please run the script SQLBackupSetup01.sql in order to follow along with the examples for this chapter. All scripts mentioned in this chapter may be found in the "Solution Series" section at www.Joes2Pros.com.*

We will need to run a stored procedure that will create yearly filegroups for the years 2006 – 2012. Next, it will create new data files per year and will assign each file to its respective filegroup. Lastly, it will create a partition function and move the data in the SalesInvoice table within the JProCo database based on the OrderDate column. Since the SalesInvoice data will not be updating previous years, we will set the filegroups <= 2011 to read only.

A database can have many filegroups but let's start by showing that most databases start with a single filegroup called PRIMARY and a single MDF file and LDF file. Right-click on **JProCo** and select **Properties**. (Figure 8.1)

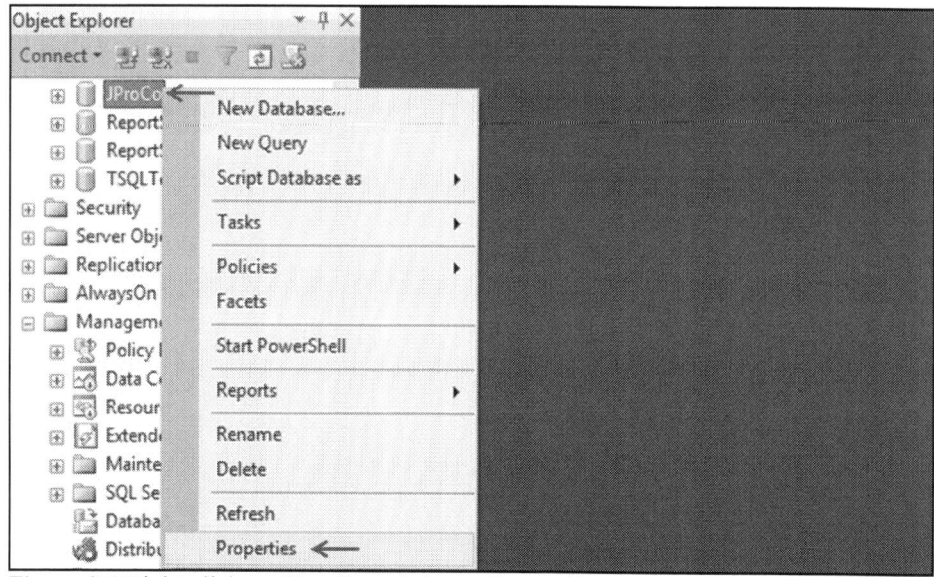

Figure 8.1 Right-click on **JProCo** and choose **Properties**.

Next, click on the **Files** page. Figure 8.2 and we will see that we have only two files: our JProCo data file in the PRIMARY filegroup and the JProCo_log file.

Chapter 8 File and Filegroup

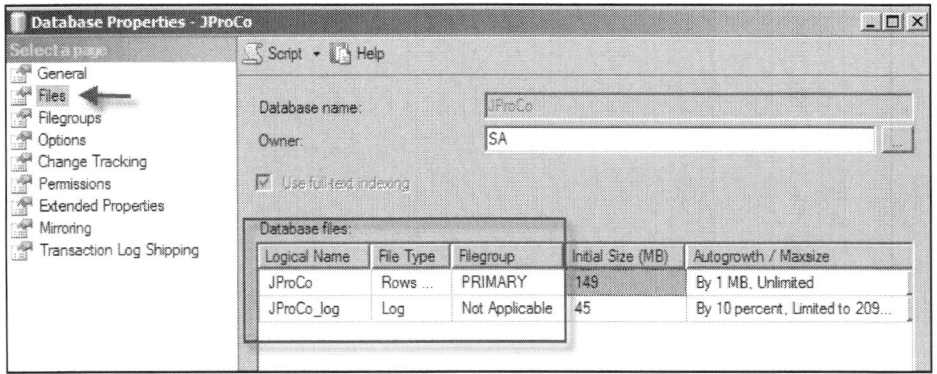

Figure 8.2 The **Files** page shows two database files, Primary data and the JProCo log file.

If we click on the **Filegroups** page (Figure 8.3) we will see that we only have one filegroup called **PRIMARY**.

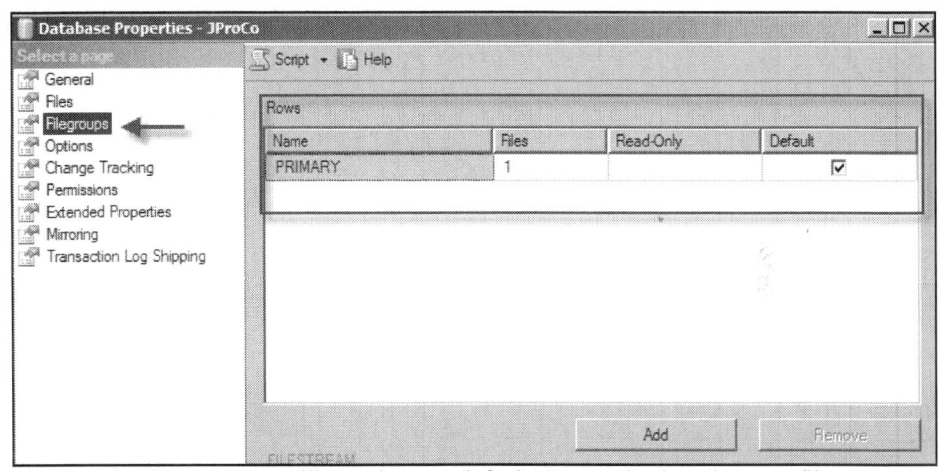

Figure 8.3 Filegroups page illustrating our default JProCo database has one file group.

Click **OK** or **Cancel** to get back to the main SSMS page. Now that we know how a default database is configured, let's run the stored procedure that will create the additional filegroups, and data files and also partition our data:

```
EXEC JProCo.[dbo].[Chapter8]
```

Chapter 8 File and Filegroup

Now repeat the steps above to review the files and filegroups and we will see the additional file and filegroups. (Figure 8.4 and Figure 8.5)

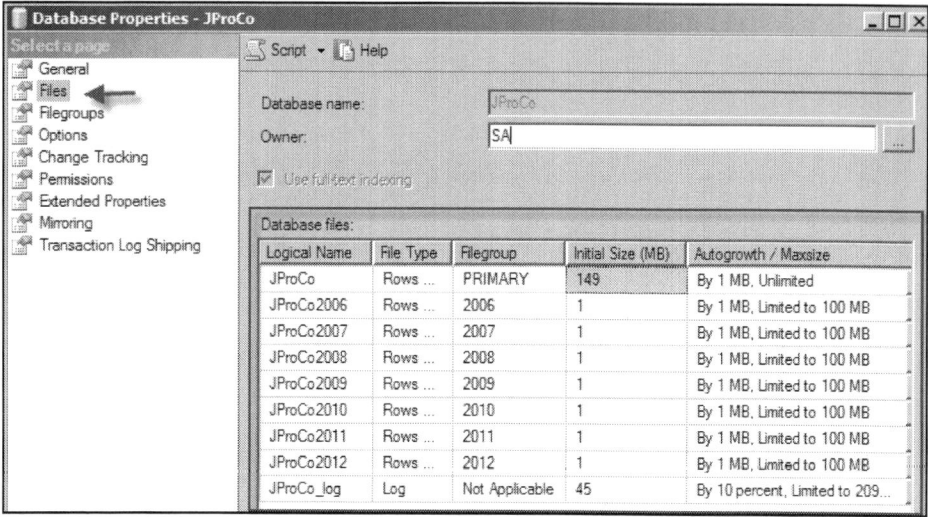

Figure 8.4 Additional files after partitioning.

Click on the **Filegroups** page. (Figure 8.5)

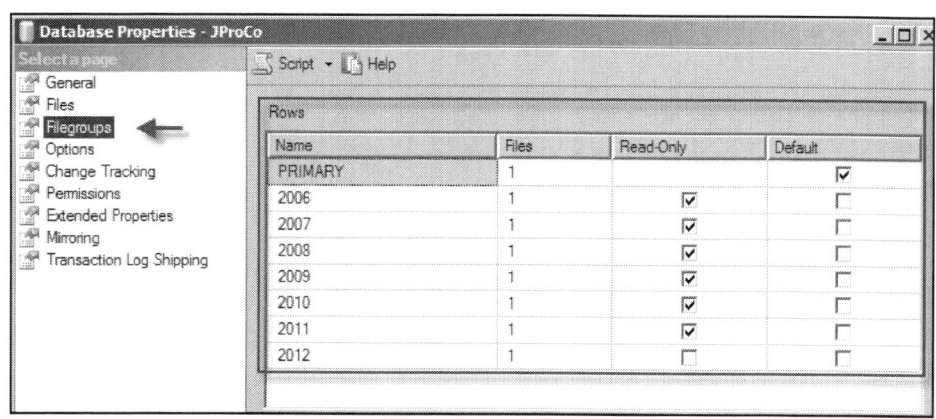

Figure 8.5 Filegroups page showing the number of filegroups we added.

We are now ready to start performing backups and restores of our files and filegroups.

Chapter 8 File and Filegroup

Using the Graphical UI

Making a full backup of a database with multiple filegroups is not very different than what we covered in Chapter 3. First right-click on the database to backup and choose **Tasks** > then the **Back Up...** option . Do this now with JProCo. (Figure 8.6)

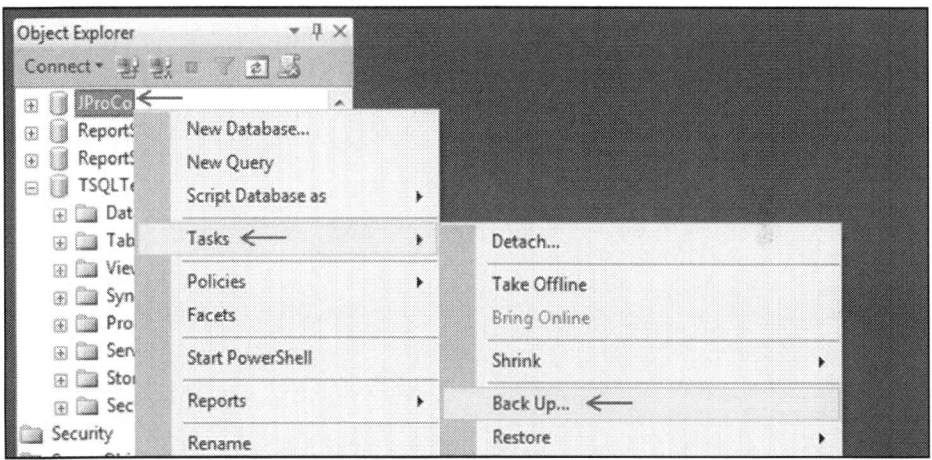

Figure 8.6 Right-click on **JProCo** > **Tasks** > **Backup**.

Once we have chosen **Back Up...** , the **General** dialog box appears where we can make a number of selections. For now do not make any changes until instructed. If we were to select **OK** at this point, it will make a full backup of the database into the default backup location for the SQL Server instance. In Figure 8.7 the first option is to choose the database we want to backup. Next is the backup type we wish to make, in this case we want full (like we did in Chapter 3) however we could make a differential like we covered in Chapter 4. There is an option for **Copy-only Backup** that we covered in Chapter 7. For **Backup component** we will select **Files and filegroups**, which will prompt a screen for us to select which file or filegroup to backup. (Figure 8.8) Under backup set we can specify the **Name** of the backup set, typically we would just accept the default value here. The next item is the destination and name of the backup file. The default path is set at the instance level. For SQL 2012 the default location is:

C:\Program Files\Microsoft SQL Server\MSSQL11.MSSQLSERVER\MSSQL\Backup\.

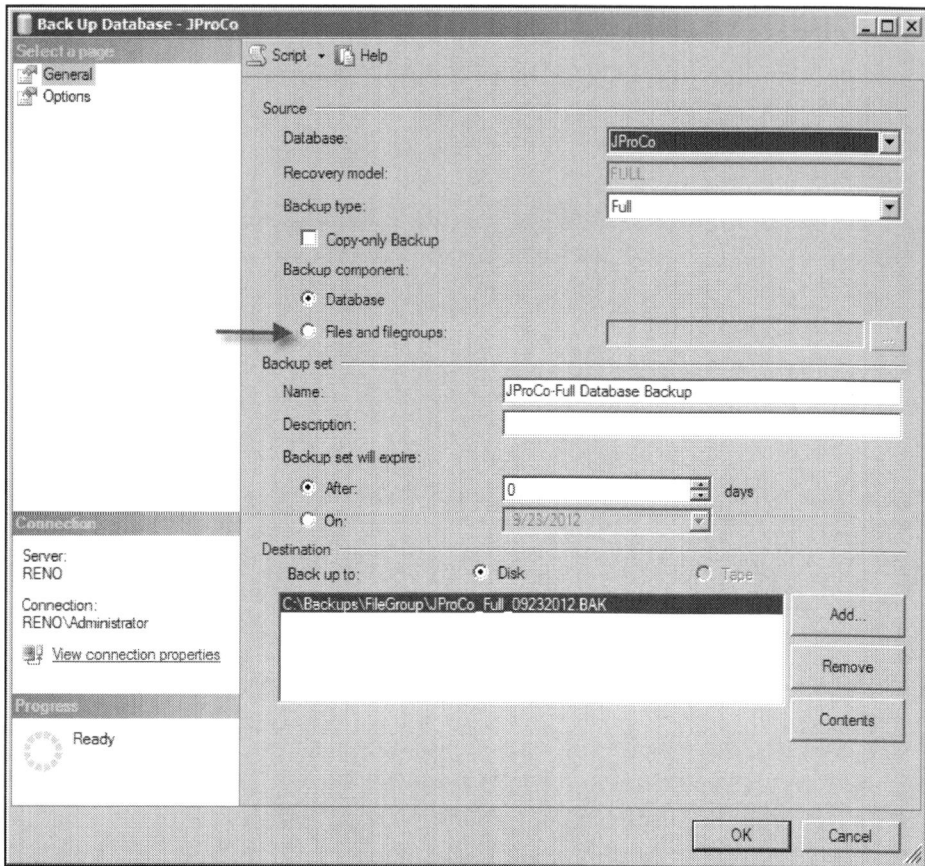

Figure 8.7 Check the radio button for **Files and filegroups**.

While following along doing these steps, click the **Files and filegroups** radio button of the **Backup component** section. After clicking the ellipsis button the window from Figure 8.8 will open. Let's choose to back up the JProCo, JProCo2008, and JProCo2006. The reason we are choosing the PRIMARY data file is that we must restore the primary in order to bring the database online.

Chapter 8 File and Filegroup

Figure 8.8 Select the files or filegroups we want to backup.

Click **OK** to complete the selection. We will now be back to Figure 8.7. To change the backup path click **Remove** > **Add** and type the path and name to use for database backup file. Figure 8.9 Just like with all other backups, it is still a best practice to have a date and time included in the backup name in addition to the backup type. As we are aware by now, there are many types of backups to make so it is very helpful having the name of the database included in the backup file name. In this example we should change the backup file name to:

C:\Backups\JProCo_File_MMDDYYYY.BAK.

In the real world if we had jobs that backed up different files on different days it would be beneficial to include information about which files were being backed up in the name as well.

Chapter 8 File and Filegroup

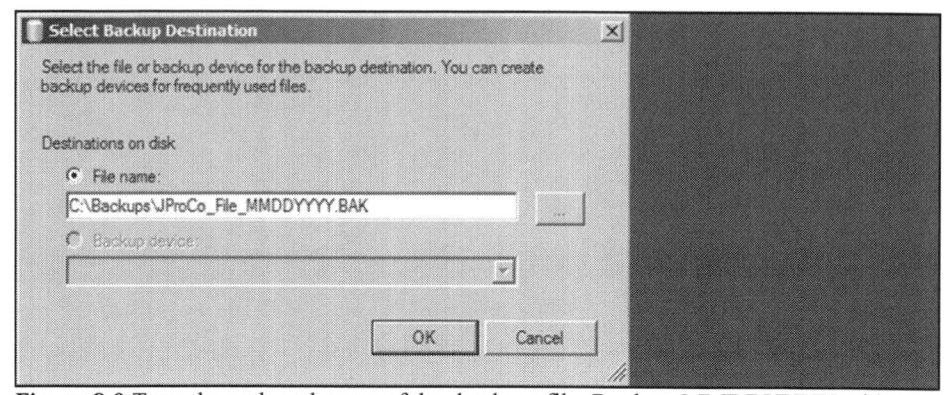

Figure 8.9 Type the path and name of the database file. Replace MMDDYYYY with actual date value in the form of Month Day Year.

Click the **Options** page and we will see that we have several more options as we did in Chapter 3 on full backups. In Figure 8.10 we will see the default values. **Overwrite media** defaults to **Append to the existing backup set**. Just like with full backups, file and filegroup backups must be verified by restoring them regularly. It is still recommend to **Verify backup when finished** however that does not mean the backup file is 100% valid. If the backup solution includes file and filegroup backups, the restore validation should also include restoring from them. Compression is also an option with **File and filegroup backups** and performs the same way as it does with full backups. With filegroup backups it is especially important that everyone in the database group be familiar with how to recover if doing file or filegroup level backups. It would also be a great idea to have a documented process for restoring these environments.

Once the selections have been made click **OK** to perform the backup to:

C:\Backups\JProCo_File_MMDDYYYY.BAK.

Don't forget that in order to perform a restore, we will need a transaction log backup as well.

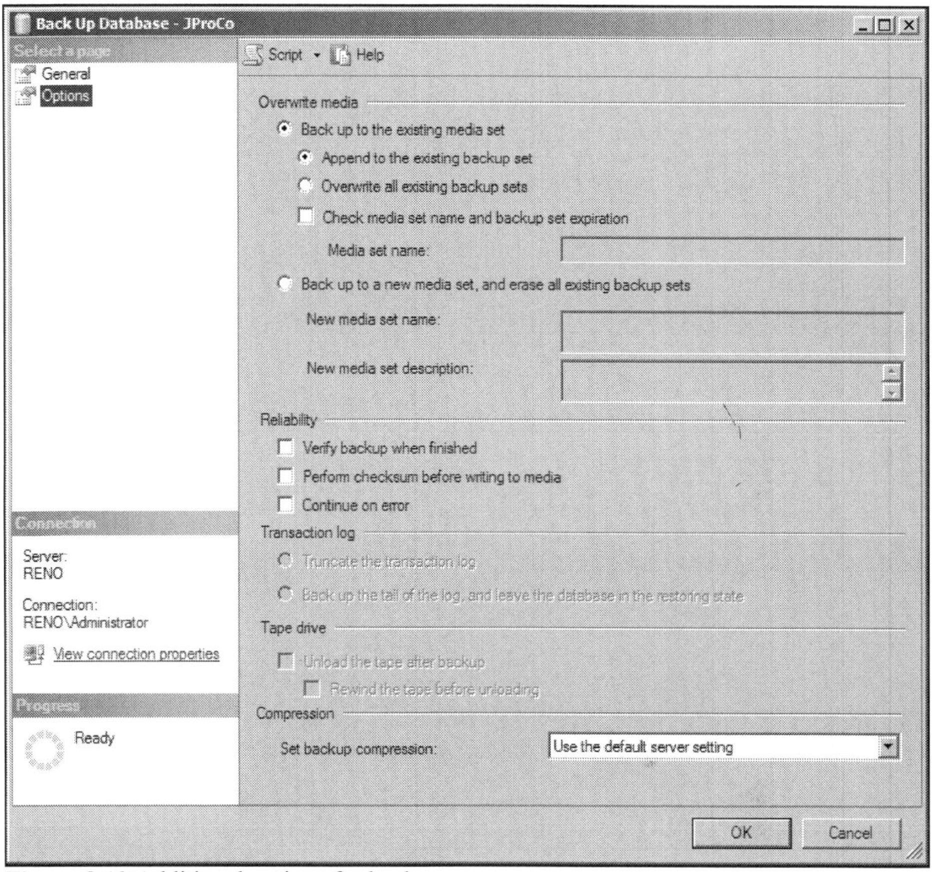

Figure 8.10 Additional options for backups.

Using T-SQL

By now we have had to notice that the preferred method for making backups is to use T-SQL. Never has it been truer than with file and filegroup backups. As we noticed in the previous section there were quite a few boxes we had to check to successfully make a backup. Having all these settings in a script makes it much easier for us to recreate the same backup consistently.

The syntax is very straightforward. We specify:

BACKUP DATABASE" DB_NAME <file or filegroup> TO backup_device WITH <OPTIONS>

We will include _TSQL at the end of the file name to not append to the file we created using the graphical UI. Let's execute the following code:

```
BACKUP DATABASE [JProCo]
  FILEGROUP = 'PRIMARY',
  FILEGROUP = '2008',
  FILEGROUP = '2006'
  TO DISK = 'C:\Backups\JProCo_File_MMDDYYYY_TSQL.BAK'
```

READER NOTE: This will only work if you ran the EXEC JProCo.[dbo].[Chapter8] code from earlier.

Restoring Using the Graphical UI

Using the graphical UI is not an option for a piecemeal restore. It can only be done using code.

Restoring Using T-SQL

T-SQL is the only option for restoring one file or filegroup at a time. We can use the graphical UI to perform a restore of all filegroups, which is essentially a full restore.

In order to bring the database online we will have to have a transaction log backup unless we perform a partial restore. For our example we will use the NO_RECOVERY option that will put our database in a restoring state. This readies our database so we can begin our restore.

So that we can also bring the entire database online, we will perform a full backup of the modified JProCo database. Our sequence of events will be 1) backup the entire database, 2) backup our primary, 2006 and 2008 filegroups, 3) insert a new record, 4) make a transaction log backup, 5) restore our PRIMARY, 2006 and 2008 filegroups. Let's go ahead and execute the following statements:

```sql
USE MASTER
GO

BACKUP DATABASE JProCo TO DISK =
  'C:\Backups\JProCo_Full_FileDemo_MMDDYYYY.BAK'
GO

BACKUP DATABASE [JProCo]
  FILEGROUP = '2006',
  FILEGROUP = 'PRIMARY',
  FILEGROUP = '2008'
TO DISK = 'C:\Backups\JProCo_File_MMDDYYYY_TSQL.BAK'
WITH INIT
GO

INSERT  INTO JProCo.[dbo].[Contractor]
  ([LastName],
  [FirstName],
  [HireDate],
  [LocationID])
VALUES ( 'Wong', 'Muhammad', '2012-04-18', '1')
GO

BACKUP LOG JProCo TO DISK =
  'C:\Backups\JProCo_TLOG_TAIL.TRN'
WITH NORECOVERY
GO

RESTORE DATABASE JProCo FILE = 'JProCo'
FROM DISK = 'C:\Backups\JProCo_File_MMDDYYYY_TSQL.BAK'
WITH PARTIAL, REPLACE, NORECOVERY
GO

RESTORE LOG JProCo FROM DISK =
  'C:\Backups\JProCo_TLOG_TAIL.TRN'
WITH RECOVERY
GO

RESTORE DATABASE JProCo FILE = N'JProCo2006'
FROM DISK =
  N'C:\Backups\JProCo_File_MMDDYYYY_TSQL.BAK'
```

```
WITH RECOVERY
GO

RESTORE DATABASE JProCo FILE = N'JProCo2008'
FROM DISK =
  N'C:\Backups\JProCo_File_MMDDYYYY_TSQL.BAK'
WITH RECOVERY
GO
```

READER NOTE: *This code will only run if you have done all the backup steps and remember to change the file names of MMDDYYYY to what you used.*

We can now check the state of each of our database files by executing the following script:

```
SELECT name, state_desc
FROM JProCo.sys.database_files
```

In Figure 8.11 we will see that the JProCo, JProCo2006, JProCo2008 files and the log are ONLINE while the rest are RECOVERY_PENDING

	name	state_desc
1	JProCo	ONLINE
2	JProCo_log	ONLINE
3	JProCo2006	ONLINE
4	JProCo2007	RECOVERY_PENDING
5	JProCo2008	ONLINE
6	JProCo2009	RECOVERY_PENDING
7	JProCo2010	RECOVERY_PENDING
8	JProCo2011	RECOVERY_PENDING
9	JProCo2012	RECOVERY_PENDING

Figure 8.11 Our JProCo, JProCo2006 and JProCo2008 files are ONLINE.

In the real world this is where things would get interesting if the system is not set up in a way to support a partial restore. For instance, if the users have an interface where they can select a date range to search on and they put in a date such as >= '2006-01-01', what will happen when the query is executed? Go ahead and run the following query:

```
SELECT * FROM JProCo.dbo.SalesInvoice
WHERE OrderDate >= '2006-01-01'
```

This gets an error message similar to the one below that states the filegroup 2007 cannot be accessed because it is offline. In situations like this it would be helpful to limit the user's ability to search outside of the boundary of data that is online. In some cases an application may be using a VIEW we could alter to limit the date range. Other systems might use a stored procedure. In most cases however we may just have to communicate to our users to use a date boundary.

```
Messages
Msg 679, Level 16, State 1, Line 1
One of the partitions of index '' for table
                                                                    0 rows
```

In the case of using a date boundary, how would the same result set look? Let's execute a few more queries to find out:

```
SELECT *
FROM JProCo.dbo.SalesInvoice
WHERE OrderDate >=
   '2008-01-01' AND OrderDate <= '2008-12-31'

SELECT *
FROM JProCo.dbo.SalesInvoice
WHERE OrderDate >=
   '2006-01-01' AND OrderDate <= '2006-12-31'

SELECT *
FROM JProCo.dbo.SalesInvoice
WHERE OrderDate >= '2012-01-01'
```

In the examples above, each query returns a set of results with no errors. Since we are restricting our date ranges to data that resides in our ONLINE filegroups SQL Server can find our data and return it without error.

Let's now restore our remaining filegroups to bring our database 100% back online. Since we are using Developer Edition we have the same features as Enterprise Edition so this is an ONLINE operation. Execute the following statements:

```
RESTORE DATABASE JProCo
  FILE = N'JProCo2007',
  FILE = N'JProCo2009',
  FILE = N'JProCo2010',
  FILE = N'JProCo2011',
  FILE = N'JProCo2012'
FROM DISK =
  'C:\Backups\JProCo_Full_FileDemo_MMDDYYYY.BAK'
WITH RECOVERY
RESTORE LOG JProCo FROM DISK =
  'C:\Backups\JProCo_TLOG_TAIL.TRN'
WITH RECOVERY
```

If we now run the script to view the **state_desc** we will see all the filegroups ONLINE as in. Figure 8.12

	name	state_desc
1	JProCo	ONLINE
2	JProCo_log	ONLINE
3	JProCo2006	ONLINE
4	JProCo2007	ONLINE
5	JProCo2008	ONLINE
6	JProCo2009	ONLINE
7	JProCo2010	ONLINE
8	JProCo2011	ONLINE
9	JProCo2012	ONLINE

Figure 8.12 All filegroups are now ONLINE.

We can now query the database again for data >= 2006 as we did before and this time we will not receive an error. Run the following script to verify:

Chapter 8 File and Filegroup

```
SELECT * FROM JProCo.dbo.SalesInvoice
WHERE OrderDate >= '2006-01-01'
```

Summary

Being able to restore portions of a database can have a huge advantage in a disastrous time. Think about these very large companies that process 10s of thousands of monetary transactions per minute. If they generate 100k an hour in revenue from their online system then they are losing that much money every minute the system is down. Do the math and you can see that every hour they are down is costing more than someone's entire year salary. Being able to get the primary data online to service the customers is critical. Piecemeal and partial restores give us that ability but it comes with a price of being much more complex to manage. If the organization utilizes file or filegroup backups, then we need to dedicate time to practicing the restore of that system until we are extremely comfortable.

Utilizing file or filegroup backups enables DBAs to perform backups of VLDBs quickly to ensure they are performed during maintenance windows so the I/O associated with backups does not impact users during production hours. In addition to providing flexibility with backups and restores, it enables DBAs to place the different files or filegroups on different sets of disks. These many disks working for you help to improve performance of disk I/O.

Before immediately jumping to the conclusion that we should partition or split a database into multiple file groups, check to make sure we are not storing data that has aged past the retention period for that type of data. Many systems log activity that is no longer needed and can be routinely purged.

When performing a file or filegroup restore we must have the accompanying transaction log backups in order to roll forward each file backup.

Have you ever seen a tag on a product that says "Warranty void if seal broken"? It's OK to use the product but certain areas of the product are not for the consumer to touch. As database administrators we will be supporting the database for many third party products. These vendors create their databases to support their products. We are tasked with making sure the data is backed up, indexes are optimized and anything else we can do to make this system perform as well as it can. In some cases there are certain areas only our vendor is authorized to change according to the agreement.

Most vendors will allow DBAs to create additional indexes to help the system run better with the understanding that those indexes may be lost when the application is upgraded in the future. This is due to some vendors dropping indexes and recreating them during their upgrade process. When we start looking at partitioning data and splitting data across multiple filegroups, these vendors many not understand or support our decision to do this. In this case they may take a stance that says if these actions are performed they will no longer support the system. This can put us in a very bad situation.

A good practice is to work with the vendors with anything we do that will alter their database. There are countless cases where DBAs have presented vendors with solutions to tune or tweak their systems that the vendors have adapted into their products. At the end of the day the vendor is just another group of technologists trying to earn a living just like any of us.

Points to Ponder
File and Filegroup Backup

1. Piecemeal restores allow us to bring up the most critical parts of our database first rather than waiting for the entire database to be fully restored.
2. To do a piecemeal restore SQL Server does File and Filegroup restores.
3. Transaction log backups are required in order to bring the database to a consistent state.
4. File and filegroup restores can only be applied to the databases in which they belong.

Chapter 8 File and Filegroup

5. You cannot attach a single file of a database if the database has multiple data files. If SQL cannot locate every file of the database the attach process fails.

Review Quiz – Chapter Eight

1.) Online piecemeal restores are available in which editions of SQL Server?
- ☐ a. Standard Edition
- ☐ b. Express Edition
- ☐ c. Enterprise Edition
- ☐ d. Developer Edition

2.) VLDB is the acronym for which phrase?
- O a. Very Large Database
- O b. Voluminous Long Data Block
- O c. Variable Elongated Database
- O d. Very Large Dense Backup

3.) It is necessary to have an accompanying transaction log when performing file-based restores.
- O a. TRUE
- O b. FALSE

Answer Key

1.) Online operations such as a piecemeal restore are an Enterprise Edition feature and are also available in Developer Edition, therefore (c) and (d) are both correct answers.

2.) VLDB is the acronym for Very Large Database, therefore (a) is the correct answer.

3.) A transaction log is in fact needed to perform the roll-forward operations during a file-based restore, therefore (a) is the correct answer.

Chapter 9. Backing Up System Databases

We take many things in life for granted such as running water, electricity, and food available in supermarkets. Most people keep some supply of extra food in their pantry and refrigerators, some purchase generators for emergencies. When bad weather is coming people stock up on water and other supplies. Just like in life, we can't always depend on systems operating as normal at all times. SQL Server should not be any different. SQL Server has several "system" databases that perform all sorts of critical things for our environment that we take for granted. These databases need special consideration when planning backup and recovery processes. We have spent many chapters discussing backing up and restoring databases. Our emphasis has been on user databases (non-system). Anyone who has spent time with SQL Server will know that there are several key system databases that are installed that have different uses. Figure 9.1 shows a list of the SQL 2012 system databases.

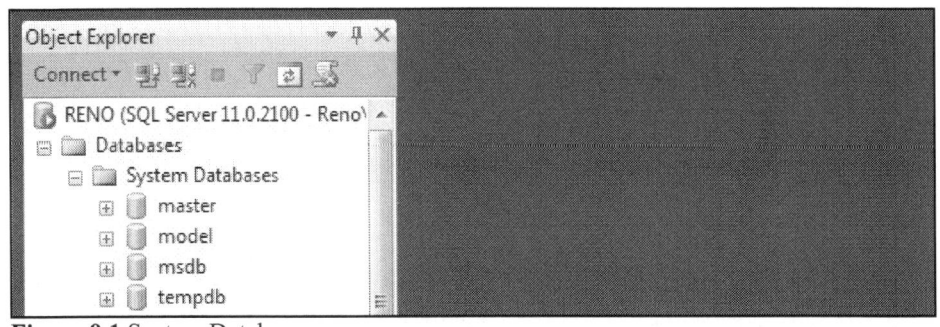

Figure 9.1 System Databases

Each system database has a key function. The master database holds SQL Server's metadata, security objects such as users, DMOs, and more. Msdb holds all backup history, job history, DTS or SSIS packages and more. Tempdb is used for many system functions such as snapshots, database mail, service broker, and all sorts of temporary objects. Model is the template database that all databases are based off of when created. This is very important for tempdb since it is recreated based off the model database each time SQL Service is restarted.

Backing up system databases is not any different than backing up user databases and in fact, system databases should be included in the regular backup routine. The only exception is tempdb. There is no need to backup tempdb nor can this even be done. This leaves master, model, and msdb to worry about being able to backup and restore. Since their backup is no different than user databases we will skip any demonstration on backups and jump right into how to restore each database beginning with master.

Restoring the Master Database

Most everyone today has a cell phone that has a countless number of contacts stored on it. We don't memorize all those numbers and most of us do not keep a written version of our contact list and numbers. If we happened to lose our cellphone or it simply dies, how easily could we return to normalcy after replacing our phone? Getting a new phone does not mean we need to retype all our numbers. This is because outside the physical phone itself most people are now storing their contacts on the providers' network. When we get a new phone all our contacts are restored to the new phone.

The master database is sort of like our contact list for our phone in that it stores a list of users that have access to our databases. If we had to rebuild a SQL Server and restore the user databases there is still more to do. Until we re-create the users on the server and granted permissions, our users cannot access the data. Nobody should know all users and passwords in order to add them all to another server in the event of a disaster.

To eliminate this risk, we backup the master database as part of our normal backup routine. The difficulty comes in with being able to restore the master database. To get started we will need to back up the master database so go ahead and execute the follow code:

```
BACKUP DATABASE MASTER TO DISK = 'C:\Backups\MASTER.BAK'
```

One of the most important considerations when restoring the master database is that the server we are restoring to must be running the same version of SQL Server down to the build number (patch level). If we are not in the habit of documenting the patch level of the SQL Server instances after every patch cycle then don't worry, it is very easy to determine this by restoring the header of the master database.

Execute the following script to find the Major.Minor.Build version:

```
RESTORE HEADERONLY FROM DISK = 'C:\Backups\MASTER.BAK'
```

The columns that reveal the version of SQL Server are SoftwareVersionMajor, SoftwareVersionMinor, and SoftwareVersionBuild. The columns are fairly self-explanatory. SQL Server versioning is Major.Minor.Build. At the time of this book the version in the demos is 11.0.2100.

Since SQL Server uses the master database we can't just open up SSMS and type a RESTORE command and overwrite the system database. There are specific steps we must take which involves starting the instance of SQL Server in single user mode in order to restore the master database. We can either start SQL Server in single user mode by using the startup parameter "-m" or use SQLCMD with a "/m". Using SQLCMD is very straightforward and it is very easy to follow along with, so for this demo we will use SQLCMD.

To start SQL Server in single user mode using SQLCMD we must first stop the SQL Server service of the instance we need to restore. Since we will be using SQLCMD let us go ahead and open a command prompt and navigate to the BINN directory of the SQL Server instance. To open a command prompt click **Start** > **Run** > type **CMD** and click **OK**. A black dialog box will open similar to Figure 9.2.

Chapter 9 Backing Up System Databases

```
Administrator: C:\Windows\system32\CMD.exe
Microsoft Windows [Version 6.1.7601]
Copyright (c) 2009 Microsoft Corporation. All rights reserved.

C:\Users\Administrator>
```

Figure 9.2 Illustration of a command prompt.

Once you have the command prompt open type **CD** and press **Enter**. This will take you to the root of the CD drive, the equivalent of clicking the folder up button in Windows Explorer. Next we want to change directories to the BINN directory of SQL Server. On SQL Server 2012 when installing into the default directory it will be C:\Program Files\Microsoft SQL Server\MSSQL11.MSSQLSERVER\MSSQL\Binn. Other versions of SQL Server will have a very similar path with a different version number. In order to change to this directory in the command prompt you will need to type **CD Program Files\Microsoft SQL Server\MSSQL11.MSSQLSERVER\MSSQL\Binn** and press **Enter**. Once you perform that step you should have a command prompt that looks similar to Figure 9.3.

```
Administrator: C:\Windows\system32\CMD.exe
Microsoft Windows [Version 6.1.7601]
Copyright (c) 2009 Microsoft Corporation. All rights reserved.

C:\Users\Administrator>cd\
C:\>CD Program Files\Microsoft SQL Server\MSSQL11.MSSQLSERVER\MSSQL\Binn
C:\Program Files\Microsoft SQL Server\MSSQL11.MSSQLSERVER\MSSQL\Binn>
```

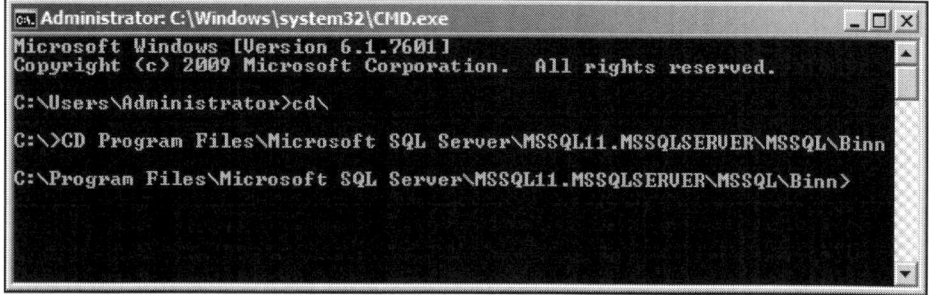

Figure 9.3 Command Prompt in the BINN directory of SQL Server.

To stop the default SQL Server instance we need to type **net stop mssqlserver** and press **Enter**.

`net stop mssqlserver`

To start SQL Server in single user mode type **net start mssqlserver /m** and press **Enter**.

```
net start mssqlserver /m
```

Next type SQLCMD and press enter.

Now that SQL is running in single user mode we can restore the master database by executing the following code. Type this all out on one line:

```
RESTORE DATABASE MASTER FROM DISK =
   'C:\Backups\MASTER.BAK' WITH REPLACE
```

One you press **Enter**, you will be prompted with a second line, type **GO** and press **Enter**. (Figure 9.4)

```
C:\Program Files\Microsoft SQL Server\MSSQL11.MSSQLSERVER\MSSQL\Binn>net start m
ssqlserver /m
The SQL Server (MSSQLSERVER) service is starting.
The SQL Server (MSSQLSERVER) service was started successfully.

C:\Program Files\Microsoft SQL Server\MSSQL11.MSSQLSERVER\MSSQL\Binn>SQLCMD
1> RESTORE DATABASE MASTER FROM DISK = 'C:\Backups\MASTER.BAK' WITH REPLACE
2> GO
Processed 424 pages for database 'MASTER', file 'master' on file 1.
Processed 3 pages for database 'MASTER', file 'mastlog' on file 1.
The master database has been successfully restored. Shutting down SQL Server.
SQL Server is terminating this process.
C:\Program Files\Microsoft SQL Server\MSSQL11.MSSQLSERVER\MSSQL\Binn>
```

Figure 9.4 Restoring the master database in a command prompt.

The master database will restore and the SQL Server instance will be shutdown. To start SQL Service back up we can type, **net start mssqlserver** again and press enter.

Restoring the msdb Database

Big executives in large corporations have executive assistants to help them stay organized. The assistants will remind the executives of where they are supposed to be, important meeting times, a spouse's anniversary, birthdays, and anything else important. These executives become dependent on their assistants for many of their day-to-day tasks. For our database servers this helpful assistant is SQL Server Agent. SQL Server Agent is the scheduler for all the jobs that run on our SQL Server instance.

These jobs may perform our database maintenance, run complex SSIS packages or other important processes. We grow dependent on the processes running on schedule and without issue. Many of these jobs and the times they run are stored with msdb along with our backup history. Let's take a moment and backup msdb by executing the following code:

```
BACKUP DATABASE MSDB TO DISK = 'C:\Backups\MSDB.BAK'
```

Almost all of SQL automation will be using msdb. That is mostly true unless we have every job scripted out and our SSIS and DTS packages stored in a version control system somewhere. Absent of that we will need to recover this data from msdb. If we are doing an in-place restore or rebuilding the instance on another piece of hardware, we can just restore the msdb database to get it back online. To restore msdb we can follow either of the restore options in Chapter 3. For this example we will use T-SQL, go ahead and execute the follow script:

```
RESTORE DATABASE MSDB FROM DISK =
  'C:\Backups\MSDB.BAK' WITH REPLACE
```

Restoring the model Database

In our industrialized society, few things are handmade. If something is to be repeated or mass-produced, we typically create a template or a mold of it to easily and consistently repeat the task. SQL Server was built that way too. SQL Server is built to hold databases and when new databases are created we want them to maintain certain characteristics. New databases should all be created to a certain standard, a default configuration. The template that SQL Server uses is the model database.

Any changes that were made to the model database will be reflected in any new databases that are created. If we change the default size of the data file and log file or the percentage of growth, then when we create a new database it will have those settings.

The model database is critical for SQL Server since tempdb is recreated each time SQL Server is restarted. If we do not have a model database,

Chapter 9 Backing Up System Databases

then SQL Server cannot create tempdb and without tempdb, SQL Server will not start.

Backing up the model database is just like backing up master and msdb. Let's go ahead and make a backup using the following script:

```
BACKUP DATABASE MODEL TO DISK = 'C:\Backups\MODEL.BAK'
```

We can restore model just as we did previously with msdb. We can also use the graphical UI or T-SQL. For this exercise we will use T-SQL to execute the following script:

```
RESTORE DATABASE MODEL FROM DISK =
  'C:\Backups\MODEL.BAK' WITH REPLACE
```

Restoring the model database in the event of a disaster where we are rebuilding a database is almost optional. It is very simple to restore it, but unless we have made changes from the default install then there is no need. If we are following best practices then surely we have made a few changes to the default size and auto growth settings, however those can easily be changed manually. Most organizations account for those changes in their server build procedures.

Restoring the tempdb Database

In the 5th grade we got extra points for doing helpful things for the teacher each day. The job I did the most for my accolades was erasing the whiteboard at the end of each class. The teacher worked all day at putting data up on the board relating to our lessons so why was he happy when I cleaned it off each day? This is because the next day a new class lesson meant a new work area with new data. Also, sometimes the teacher would erase half the board in the middle of the day to make some corrections to the data. We can say the whiteboard was like a thinking area for data that was using our real-time workflow. SQL can also put its ideas and temporary work on its own whiteboard area. This data work area is the tempdb. None of its contents is officially stored or has any long-term relevancy to the other databases. Tempdb is just like a SQL whiteboard or scratch paper.

Since tempdb is recreated each time on a SQL Server restart, there is no need to backup and restore tempdb. As a matter of fact, backing up tempdb is not even an option. Go ahead and try by executing the following script:

```
BACKUP DATABASE TempDB TO DISK =
  'C:\Backups\TempDB.BAK'
```

The following error should have been received:

```
Messages
Msg 3147, Level 16, State 3, Line 1
Backup and restore operations are not allowed on database TempDB.
Msg 3013, Level 16, State 1, Line 1
BACKUP DATABASE is terminating abnormally.

                                                          0 rows
```

Summary

Over the years, reading blog posts, answering questions on forums, and speaking at SQL events, a common story has been told. The story involves data professionals that suffer a production crash that involves bringing up their systems on a new server. Once the data professional installs SQL Server and restores their user databases none of the applications or users can connect. The DBA quickly realizes all the users are stored in the master database and they have to rush to restore it as well. What the DBA is lacking is the knowledge and experience in restoring the master database. When they try to restore the master database they find that the install of SQL Server is not at the same patch level so now they have to download updates to get it to the same level. Once they overcome that issue and get master restored users and applications are able to connect.

The DBA at this point feels good that the system is up. They boast in the glory that they saved the day. However, the next day they come in to work and find a new problem being reported. None of the ETL jobs ran last night. The DBA forgot that all the jobs and packages are stored in the msdb database so now they have to restore msdb and manually run each job to get the system caught up. System databases each perform a unique service to SQL Server. Each database with the exception of tempdb should be part of our regular backup routine to ensure that we can fully recover those critical databases. Once all the jobs process, the system returns to normal and business goes on as usual.

Had this DBA practiced doing a full system restore, they would have saved their company hours of downtime and lost productivity.

System databases are a critical part of SQL Server and all but tempdb should be backed up in our regular backup routine. Master, model and msdb are backed up just like a user database and model and msdb are restored like user databases as well. The master database must be restored in single user mode and requires the SQL Server instance to be at the same build level as the backup. This can present extra steps when trying to recover a system. The tempdb database is recreated each time SQL Server service is started; therefore it cannot be backed up and restored.

Points to Ponder
Backing Up System Databases

1. A major part of the restore strategy for a SQL Server instance should be recovering data that is stored in Master and msdb. Being able to successfully restore a user database but not having any users configured with permissions will not enable any productivity.

2. If the master database is damaged to where we cannot start up SQL, we can perform a rebuild.

3. Due to SQL Server having to be on the same version in order to restore, it is best practice to have all the service packs and installation media available on the network. In times of a disaster, the Internet may not be available for us to download from MSDN.

Review Quiz – Chapter Nine

1.) The tempdb should be included in a backup routine.

O a. TRUE
O b. FALSE

2.) The model database is the template for new database creations.

O a. TRUE
O b. FALSE

3.) SQL Server must be in single user mode in order to restore the master database.

O a. TRUE
O b. FALSE

Answer Key

1.) The tempdb database cannot be backed up, therefore the answer is (b) FALSE.

2.) SQL Server uses the model database as the template for new database creations. The answer is (a) TRUE

3.) In order to restore the master database the SQL Server instance has to be at the same build level as the database, and we must start SQL Server in single user mode. The answer is (a) TRUE.

Chapter 10. Additional Best Practices

Anyone who owns a car knows there is much more to owning and operating a car than just knowing how to drive. There are many maintenance tasks that need to be performed that your car may not alert you to. This needed maintenance helps to keep your vehicle running smooth and extends the life of the automobile. Some of the tasks (if not maintained) could endanger your car's life span. Things such as changing the oil, rotating the tires, replacing air filters, checking tire pressure and the list can go on.

Being responsible for SQL Server and recovering databases is much like owning a car. There are several additional maintenance tasks or best practices that we need to follow in order to have a smooth running server and prolong our career.

The following topics are several additional items that every DBA should be aware of for best practices.

DBCC CHECKDB

Corruptions happen in daily life, especially in government and politics. Within technology, application programs have errors, hard drives crash, network switches can fail and a whole host of other problems can develop. Our databases sit on very large disks that are connected to very complex servers. Any number of bad things can happen while data is being written to the disks. Although SQL Server is extremely good at doing error handling, it can't always save us 100% of the time. When it can't, the database or a portion of it can become corrupt.

The way that we scan and check for this corruption is by running DBCC CHECKDB on our databases. This command checks the integrity of the database, both logical and physical. CHECKDB does this by running three additional checks.

1) CHECKALLOC checks the consistency of disk space allocation.
2) CHECKTABLE checks the pages and structures of the table or indexed view.
3) CHECKCATALOG checks the catalog consistency.

CHECKDB also validates Service Broker data, the content of indexed views, and link level consistency of VARBINARY(MAX) data in the file system using FILESTREAM.

It is highly recommended that we regularly run DBCC CHECKDB against all our production databases. A best practice is to have this scheduled to run as part of the regular maintenance and to output the results to a file.

If corruption is detected quickly enough, we have a much better chance of recovering it from backup or being able to repair the corruption.

Backup Encryption

Security is important. Our banks lock cash and coins away in a very secure safe. The United States government stores gold in one of the most secure places in the world. Your organization requires you to log onto the network, and probably has some form of physical security to access the building. Most enterprise SANs encrypt the higher end storage so our data that is stored on the disk is encrypted. We can require authentication to access our databases to keep the data secure. However, native SQL Server backups (when not using Transparent Data Encryption (TDE) encryption) are not encrypted. What does this mean for us? Anyone with read access to the drive that is holding our backups can make a copy and restore that database to a SQL Server running the same version or higher. Once they restore the database, if they are an SA on the new server, they have access to all the data. Who are the domain or local server administrators on your database servers? Any one of them could make a copy of that database.

What can we (as DBAs) do to protect our backups? The easiest thing to do is back up to an encrypted disk or disk share. This is great if we have that option available within our organization or if our version of SQL Server supports TDE. If this is the case then we can choose to encrypt our backups. If neither of these options is available then there are several third party tools available on the market. Several of these tools also support backup compression as well as the option to encrypt the backup files.

Someone having access to our encrypted backup files (even if someone has access to the backup) is of no risk unless they also get the encryption key/password. Without the key they cannot restore and access the data.

What is Crash Recovery

When a database is restored the first thing that happens is the file is created and initialized. This can be time consuming if the database is large and instant file initialization is not enabled. Once the file is initialized, the data is copied. The final steps are the redo and undo portion, which is called crash recovery. Any transactions that were written to the log file but not to the data file prior to the crash must be rolled forward to put the database in a consistent state. If there are transactions that were in flight and not committed before the crash, they must be rolled back.

Instant File Initialization

When you visit a financial institution to cash a check or withdraw money from your account, the teller will always count the money twice. They typically count it first for themselves and then count the money to you as they are handing it to you. This is how they guarantee that you are getting what you expect and that they don't accidently give you too much money shorting their drawer. This act of counting the money out twice gives us a sense that the teller is trustworthy. When we create a database in SQL Server, that file is created on the NTFS file system and SQL Server has to zero out each page in the file. This can be a very time consuming task.

In SQL Server 2005 and above on Windows Server 2003 and above we can enable instant file initialization. This is turned on by going into **Security Settings > Local Policies > User Rights Assignment > Perform Volume Maintenance Tasks >** and adding our SQL service account. Now when we create a new database, expand a database file or drop and restore a database. SQL Server no longer has to zero out each page of the data file. That step is now skipped.

Summary

Checking for corruption in our databases is very important. Corruption can occur for a number of reasons but 95% of the time it is related to a hardware issue. SQL Server is very forgiving and will backup a corrupt database. Just because our database can be backed up and users can query the database does not mean everything is ok. Running DBCC CHECKDB is an integral part of database maintenance and should be on a schedule to run.

Understanding crash recovery is important to know what process a database goes through after being restored or recovered from a crash of the server. Implementing instant file initialization can drastically improve our recovery time when restoring a database to a new server or if restoring after a database has been dropped.

Encrypting backups provides great protection to preventing data breaches. If we are not encrypting our backups, discuss this with our team to ensure the risk is minimal and proper safeguards are in place.

Points to Ponder - Additional Best Practices

1. DBCC CHECKDB is very well documented on MSDN. If any errors return after running CHECKDB there are arguments (additional options) we can use with CHECKDB to dig further into the problem or possibly correct the issue.
2. Dealing with database corruption is usually not a pleasant experience. Having proper backups is the key to being able to repair and recover from corruption.
3. Protecting our backup files is just as important as protecting our databases. In some cases it may be easier for a disgruntled employee to access our backup files than the database itself.
4. Instant file initialization can drastically decrease the amount of time it takes for tempdb to be recreated when SQL Server starts. Since tempdb is recreated each time the service is started, if tempdb has been resized and is gigabytes in size, this could delay the SQL Server from being online for several minutes.
5. There is a slight security risk when enabling instant file initialization since the data file is no longer zeroed out.

Review Quiz – Chapter Ten

1.) DBCC CHECKDB performs what function in SQL Server?
- O a. It checks to make sure the database has been backed up.
- O b. It checks for consistency to find corruption.
- O c. It reorganizes indexes.
- O d. It checks to ensure database mirroring is in sync.

2.) When SQL Server makes backups, it will check for corruption and will NOT backup a corrupt database.
- O a. TRUE
- O b. FALSE

3.) Backup encryption is a feature in Standard and Enterprise editions of SQL Server and is on by default.
- O a. TRUE
- O b. FALSE

Answer Key

1.) DBCC CHECKDB checks for corruption. Therefore answer (b) is correct.

2.) SQL Server will backup corrupt databases so answer (b) is correct.

3.) Although using TDE in Enterprise edition will backup to an encrypted file, there is no "encryption" option for backups in SQL Server yet. Answer (b) is correct.

INDEX

C

CHECKALLOC, 142
CHECKCATALOG, 142
CHECKTABLE, 142
Copy Backup, 13, 14, 16, 18, 102, 104, 108
COPY_ONLY, 102, 103, 104, 105, 106, 107, 108, 109, 110
Crash Recovery, 143, 144
CREATE DATABASE, 36, 39

D

Data loss, 73, 98, 99, 100, 101
Datafiles, 23, 24, 27, 28, 29, 30, 31, 32, 34, 35, 37, 39, 40
DBCC CHECKDB, 55, 142, 144, 145, 146
Differential Backup, 11, 12, 13, 15, 16, 17, 41, 57, 58, 62, 69, 70, 71, 87, 103, 109, 110

F

file initialization, 143, 144, 145
Full/Normal Backup, 7, 8, 10, 11, 12, 13, 14, 15, 16, 17, 18, 41, 42, 47, 51, 54, 55, 57, 58, 62, 65, 68, 69, 70, 71, 73, 74, 75, 76, 79, 80, 81, 83, 87, 88, 89, 92, 94, 95, 96, 97, 99, 100, 102, 103, 104, 108, 117, 122

G

Graphical UI, 39, 41, 42, 47, 48, 54, 56, 58, 62, 68, 75, 76, 80, 81, 87, 89, 90, 91, 95, 104, 108, 122, 137

I

Incremental Backup, 9, 10, 14, 15, 16, 17, 41

L

Logfile, 23, 24, 27, 28, 29, 30, 31, 32, 33, 34, 40

M

MSSQL\DATA, 23, 30, 42, 54, 59, 68, 69, 77, 104, 118, 134

N

NORECOVERY, 53, 55, 57, 62, 68, 69, 70, 81, 87, 88, 96, 97, 99, 123

R

RECOVERY, 51, 53, 55, 57, 66, 68, 70, 85, 87, 88, 96, 97, 99, 122, 123, 124, 126
Recovery Point Objective (RPO), 92, 93, 94, 98, 100, 101
Recovery time objective (RTO), 92, 93, 98, 100
REPLACE, 51, 53, 54, 55, 56, 66, 68, 69, 85, 123, 135, 136, 137
RESTORE DATABASE, 50, 53, 54, 65, 67, 68, 69, 84, 86, 87, 88, 123, 124, 126, 135, 136, 137
Restore Strategy, 57, 92, 97, 139
Rick Morelan, 3, 4

INDEX

S

STANDBY, 53, 55, 68, 70

T

Tim Radney, 1, 3, 4
Transaction Log Backup, 73, 75, 76, 80, 89, 90, 95, 96, 97, 98, 99, 108, 109, 120, 122, 128
Transact-SQL, 6, 39, 41, 46, 47, 53, 54, 55, 56, 58, 61, 62, 68, 75, 80, 81, 87, 89, 91, 95, 107, 121, 122, 136, 137

Transparent Data Encryption, 143, 146

V

VARBINARY(), 142

W

WITH MOVE, 53, 54, 68, 69

Made in the USA
Lexington, KY
29 October 2012